WHATSOEVER THINGS ARE LOVELY

WHATSOEVER THINGS ARE LOVELY

Must-Have Accessories for God's Perfect Peace

RHONDA RHEA

Revell

a division of Baker Publishing Group
Grand Rapids, Michigan

© 2009 by Rhonda Rhea

Published by Revell
a division of Baker Publishing Group
P.O. Box 6287, Grand Rapids, MI 49516-6287
www.revellbooks.com

Printed in the United States of America

Library of Congress Cataloging-in-Publication Data
Rhea, Rhonda.
    Whatsoever things are lovely : must-have accessories for God's perfect peace / Rhonda Rhea.
        p. cm.
    Includes bibliographical references.
    ISBN 978-0-8007-3252-3 (pbk.)
    1. Christian women—Religious life. 2. Peace—Religious aspects—Christianity. I. Title.
    BV4527.R495 2009
    248.8′43—dc22   2009020395

To my mom, Elizabeth Camille,
who openhandedly introduced me to the joy of
digging through her jewelry box,
and who openheartedly introduced me to the
True Giver of perfect peace.

CONTENTS

Part 3 "Keep your minds on whatever is . . . right"

Part 4 "Keep your minds on whatever is . . . holy"

Part 5 "Keep your minds on whatever is . . . friendly and proper"

Part 6 "Don't ever stop thinking about what is truly worthwhile and worthy of praise"

ACKNOWLEDGMENTS

As ever and always, big, blinging thanks to my hubby/hero, Richie Rhea, for being such a shining example of the peace of Christ and for unwavering support, encouragement, and unconditional love and patience. How many husbands could resist making fun of a wife stressing over a book about *peace*?

Shining thank-yous to Andy Rhea (www.andyrheamusic.com), Jordan Rhea, Kaley Rhea, Allie Rhea, and Daniel Rhea for love, encouragement, inspiration—and for just being all-around wonderful people. Your love for Jesus, your amazing talents, and your sweet spirits bring great peace and joy to my blessed-mama heart!

More thanks to my faithful prayer team—what wonderful warrior women! Keeping this project bathed in prayer has been a big task and an inestimable investment. Humble, sincere thank-yous to Janet Bridgeforth, Tina Byus, Diane Campbell, Mary Clark, Theresa Easterday, Chris Hendrickson, Melinda Massey, and Peanuts Rudolph. I cherish you all!

I so appreciate the help at every corner from my favorite agent of all time, Pamela Harty, who shares my heart for ministry, and from all those at The Knight Agency who help make it possible for me to do what I love to do.

How I appreciate gifted editor Jennifer Leep—a super editor and truly super person. Big thank-yous to all those who make up the talented team at the Revell division of Baker Publishing Group. Art, marketing, publicity, editorial—every team member is such a gift. Barb Barnes even makes copyediting a joy!

A huge nod of thanks goes to Joanne Sampl of Next-Step-Up Communications, whose techy contributions are always invaluable and whose ministry counsel, web design, and marketing help keep us up and running—and whose friendship is such a great blessing.

More head-bobs of thanks to my church family at Troy First Baptist Church for prayers and encouragement, and to Halo & Wings, our local Christian bookstore here in Troy, Missouri.

Much gratitude to the Advanced Writers and Speakers Association, my heart-sisters who share support, knowledge, godly insights, and powerful prayers.

A personal thank-you to Peanuts Rudolph, assistant and friend, who not only faithfully prayed very specifically over this book, but knew exactly when to offer beautiful words of encouragement. I especially loved Peanuts' spiritual spunk the day she called to tell me that while she was praying, she started giggling. She said it was because she was overjoyed at the thought that God had already finished this book. I confess that at that point I was just hoping he was using software compatible with mine. Then I remembered that I use "Word," and that made me giggle too. It was a great reminder to keep it all funneling through, filtered by, and reflected in and from HIS "Word."

Which brings me to my truest, biggest debt of gratitude. It is ever reserved for my heavenly Father, the God of peace, and the God who gives peace. My heart is full of grateful appreciation to the God who proves again and again that he can truly use anyone. I'm so blessed to be one of his "anyone" servants.

Finally, my friends, keep your minds on whatever is true, pure, right, holy, friendly, and proper. Don't ever stop thinking about what is truly worthwhile and worthy of praise. You know the teachings I gave you, and you know what you heard me say and saw me do. So follow my example. And God, who gives peace, will be with you.

Philippians 4:8–9 CEV

INTRODUCTION

*"Keep Your Minds," . . . and All These
Blings Will Be Added unto You*

"Finally, my friends, keep your minds"

No doubt I could start a support group for the chronically over-accessorized. Bows, baubles, and bangles—rings and things and all kinds of bling—I love to accessorize.

Hello, my name is Rhonda Rhea and I'm a bling-aholic. There's a good reason I'll never start that support group, though. Recovery programs don't work for those who don't want to recover. And I'm not anywhere near willing to leave the life of over-the-top accessorizing. Is it even possible to overembellish? Not in my bling-book.

Personally, I'm continually adding more and more baubles and bangles. It's more than just the fact that you rarely have to say, "Do these earrings make me look fat?" Accessories not only add that adorable extra something that gives just the right sparkle, but they're also great smoke screens.

Cameo or Camo?

I'll confess that now that I've hit the midlife mark, these days it's not so much about *accessorizing* as it is *camouflaging*. Got things to hide? Add a little smoke-screen-sparkle here, a little diamond-decorated diversion there. In the immortal and sage words of Anita Renfroe in her book of the same title: "If you can't lose it, decorate it!"[1] It's a philosophy that helps with whatever you need to lose, as well as whatever may be sagging, bagging, or otherwise sinking slowly into the sunset.

I'll just warn you that the midlife need for accessory misdirection hits rather suddenly. It's like you get up one morning, glance in the mirror, and suddenly find a *forest troll* looking back at you. More than scary. You'd like to assume you've been magically transported to some enchanted woodland. But sadly, it's real life. In real life, you have to decide what you're going to do about that troll.

Trolling for Bling

Take it from me, a sister who's "been there, trolled that": when you find the lumpy-bumpy hobgoblin in the mirror, don't try to fight him. Trust me, trolls fight dirty. What do you do instead? You go trolling for bling.

Yes, you rifle through your jewelry box to find yourself a sparkly necklace or some other blindingly shiny, attention-grabbing piece. It's a little bling that can hopefully create a glare up the face so brilliant that no one notices any imperfections. Just the right bling can be ideally misdirecting—a helpful thing when you're talking trolls.

I say, instead of waiting for the troll to ask questions to see if you can pass over his bridge, take the lead. Distract him with earrings that are bigger than your head.

Misdirected Lives

Sadly, there's an entirely different kind of misdirection: one of a soul living in utter chaos. It's a misdirected life marked by varying combinations of discontentment, stress, fear, impurity, bitterness, frustration, unfruitfulness, selfishness, loneliness, confusion, discouragement, laziness, worry, or inconsistency—all the things that are the exact opposite of peace.

I've been blessed to meet women from one side of this country to the other. You might be surprised to find that most (not just some, but most) are struggling with at least one of the items in that peace-crushing list. And let me confess right here at the get-go that I've been there so many times, it's downright embarrassing. All too often I've chosen to live without peace in a situation where peace was waiting for me—right there for the asking.

Would you be surprised to learn that many women say peace is their number one greatest need? Every woman does need peace. And every woman desires peace—I daresay, most would even give up some of their greatest treasures in this life to gain it. But so many find that it always seems devastatingly out of reach. How can that be?

Our natural bent is to reach for that peace in all the wrong directions—to reach for all the wrong things.

Reaching for the Right Accessories

Let's get some perspective and reach in the right direction for just the right peace. Never mind the jewelry box. We can find the right peace as we understand what the Bible says about the true and lasting peace of God. When we're looking for peace, there are certain life "accessories" that are absolute must-haves. And we need to go after them "whatsoever" it might cost us!

The Bible teaches that we "wear" this life in Christ (take a look at the Colossians 3 passage at the end of this introduction). In Philippians 4:8–9, Paul gives the perfect complements to that outfit:

> Finally, my friends, keep your minds on whatever is true, pure, right, holy, friendly, and proper. Don't ever stop thinking about what is truly

worthwhile and worthy of praise. You know the teachings I gave you, and you know what you heard me say and saw me do. So follow my example. And God, who gives peace, will be with you.

CEV

The Philippians 4 passage becomes our outline for keeping our minds on those things that bring us the genuine peace every woman needs. Have you ever done something goofy, then asked yourself the question, "Where was my mind?" This passage gives us some specifics on just the right "wheres" to put our minds— and where we need to *keep* them to experience the life-altering peace of God.

Have You Lost Your Mind?

Losing our minds? That's easy. As a matter of fact, that happens to be one area where I have some pretty impressive expertise. But what can we do to "keep" our mind instead of losing it? "Keep your minds" actually means to focus and meditate on these lovely things. We're instructed here to spend some focused think-time and some focused think-energy.

Did you notice that our focus passage begins with the "finally" part of Paul's revealing message to the Philippians on how to live in peace and joy? I might also add that it's not his only "finally" in his letter—I thought I was the only one who did that. But a "finally" means that this is a summary of other important truths he's taught. He's pointing to this spot as a place to zero in. He wants his readers to walk away after reading the letter with this principle firmly under their belts—sparkly or not.

Searching through these verses, we can let the truths of Scripture zero us in on learning to "keep our mind," dwelling on the right things, those things that will bring peace. Let's reach together for the perfect peace!

Ready, Set, Embellish!

Ready to spend some time basking in and dwelling on his peace? Slip off your shoes—and your dangly earrings—pull up a chair, get comfy, and have a peace-filled read.

Or perhaps peace is something that seems absolutely unattainable at this point in your life. Busyness, doubts, troubles, sin habits, bitterness, worry—there are so many potential peace zappers. Friend, don't put this book down until you understand that the one and only way to peace is to look into the face of Christ. "Let us fix our eyes on Jesus, the author and perfecter of our faith" (Heb. 12:2). We need to fix our eyes on him before we look to anyone or anything else, or there will be no peace in this life.

> *O Lord, may we fix our eyes on you. Will you take us on a journey through this book—a journey that leads us to a deeper and sweeter knowledge of and trust in you? As we seek peace, Lord, may we seek YOU. And as we seek you, I ask that you would grant a more complete peace than ever before—a life-altering, right-down-to-the-soul peace. I ask, Father, that you would meet the deepest soul-need of every person who picks up this book, all by your grace and your mercy. Thank you that you are the God of peace. All glory and honor to you!*

Matthew 6:33 says, "But seek first the kingdom of God and His righteousness, and all these things shall be added to you" (NKJV). Need peace? Let's seek *him* and *his* kingdom. All those other things? They'll soon be just water under the troll bridge.

Do not lie to one another, for you have stripped off the old (unregenerate) self with its evil practices,

And have clothed yourselves with the new [spiritual self], which is [ever in the process of being] renewed and remolded into [fuller and more perfect knowledge upon] knowledge after the image (the likeness) of Him Who created it.

Clothe yourselves therefore, as God's own chosen ones (His own picked representatives), [who are] purified and holy and well-beloved [by God Himself, by putting on behavior marked by] tenderhearted pity and mercy, kind feeling, a lowly opinion of yourselves, gentle ways, [and] patience [which is tireless and long-suffering, and has the power to endure whatever comes, with good temper].

Be gentle and forbearing with one another and, if one has a difference (a grievance or complaint) against another, readily pardoning each other; even as the Lord has [freely] forgiven you, so must you also [forgive].

And above all these [put on] love and enfold yourselves with the bond of perfectness [which binds everything together completely in ideal harmony].

And let the peace (soul harmony which comes) from Christ rule (act as umpire continually) in your hearts [deciding and settling with finality all questions that arise in your minds, in that peaceful state] to which as [members of Christ's] one body you were also called [to live]. And be thankful (appreciative), [giving praise to God always].

Colossians 3:9–10, 12–15 AMP

PART 1

"KEEP YOUR MINDS ON WHATEVER IS TRUE"

EARBOBS OR 1
DOORKNOBS?

God's Word Is True

Do you have a pair of earrings that looks more like a pair of doorknobs than a pair of earbobs? Gotta love those plus-size accessories. It's a little embarrassing, however, to admit that I have some earrings that are bigger and jinglier than a janitor's key ring. These are the kinds of earrings that are not so much worn as they are *hauled*. If the dimensions of a pair of earrings get too close to the measurements of the mud flaps on a tractor trailer, it might be necessary to check city and state regulations before taking them out on the road without a license.

Still, I love the crazy, dangly earrings. The danglier, the better. It's like taking along a couple of friends everywhere you go. Hanging with the homegirls.

Are You Ready to Rumble?

I admit that those gals have given me trouble a few times. Catching on the shoulder of my sweater, tangling in my hair, slapping me upside the head. I have one pair that could pass for matching gongs. My ears ring for a while after I wear them. Then there was that retro pair I used to have. They were shaped like giant daisies. Those things had a power swing that nearly put an eye out. Totally the wrong kind of flower power.

If your earrings are hanging too low, wobbling to or fro, anytime you could actually tie 'em in a knot or tie 'em in a bow—and anytime they threaten any of your five senses—they're probably just a little too hazardously bulky.

A pair of earrings you could trip over? When we're in physical danger, it's not a bad idea to hire an ironworker to shear off a foot or two. Can you imagine how embarrassing it would be to get tripped up by your own bling? Sacrifice though it is, it's always safer to trim the bling a trifle to better trip-proof your life. It could save us all some big-time strife. And maybe an eye.

Just the Stumble-Proofing We're Looking For

Want to trip-proof your life spiritually? Psalm 119:165 says, "Those who love your instructions have great peace and do not stumble" (NLT[a]). Not only does God's Word keep us from tripping, but did you notice that loving his Word gives us peace? Exactly what we're looking for! And not just a little peace. Great peace.

Our focus passage in Philippians tells us to keep our minds on "whatever is true." And God's Word is the truest of every "whatever." Meditating on and understanding his promises brings a sense of serene well-being, knowing he's got us covered in every way that counts. Peace. The more we read his Word and understand how he loves us and takes care of us eternally, the more we find that sweet inner rest.

And the more we know him through his Word, the more we're able to pinpoint those things that would threaten to trip us up. As we learn more and more of his Word, we get more of his perspective and we're able to identify those tricky, peace-crushing obstacles. "My friends, keep your minds on whatever is true." What a vital passage for our lives!

No need to be blind to those obstacles that threaten to trip us. God's Word does away with blindness and shows us the way to walk out our faith-lives.

Blind Test

I was watching a commercial for some sort of miracle anti-aging face cream the other day. The announcer lady said it would undo years of sun damage and other skin woes and that researchers rated the cream "best" for results in all categories in a blind test. That got me wondering. Why would I trust a *blind* test of a skin care product? Wouldn't I want all the researchers to actually *see* the results? If someone is going to promise me that a cream is going to shore up a saggy, sun-damaged face, I want to see the shore, so to speak. Seeing is believing, right?

John 20:31 says, "But these are written [recorded], in order that you may believe that Jesus is the Christ (the Anointed One), the Son of God, and that through believing and cleaving to and trusting and relying upon Him you may have life through (in) His name [through Who He is]" (AMP).

A Word to the Wise—and to the Simple

No need to "blindly" believe. Ours is not a blind faith. We've been given God's Word, written down, so that we may believe. Psalm 119:130 says, "The teaching of your word gives light, so even the simple can understand" (NLT^b). Sounds like the opposite of blindness to me. It's light! How gracious that our heavenly Father has granted his light not just for the scholars but for the average simple gal—for me!

And he will open our minds to understand his Word. Are you thinking you need a seminary degree or special theological expertise to comprehend his Word? There's certainly nothing wrong with being educated in the things of God, but don't think for a second that's what God requires before he'll grant insight into his truth. There's one prerequisite for enlightenment in his teaching: a desire to know him more.

Take a look at what he says in Deuteronomy 32:1–2: "Listen, O heavens, and I will speak! Hear, O earth, the words that I say! Let my teaching fall on you like rain; let my speech settle like dew. Let my words fall like rain on tender grass, like gentle showers on young plants" (NLT[b]).

What kind of special degree does grass need to receive rain? Did your flowers need special training to allow you to water them? No, they didn't need a single lesson, class, or tutorial. God uses his Word like a gentle shower on a young plant. Now there's some flower power! His Word is sweet like dew. I love that picture. There's nothing a young plant needs more. There's no more perfect nourishment. His Word is the sweet rain that can wash away any spiritual blind spot.

Let It Pour

If you've been a little too casual about reading and studying God's Word, are you ready to let its sweet rain wash over you? Are you ready to have your life changed? That's exactly what will happen as you let it become part of your daily routine and part of . . . well . . . *you*. Open up your Bible with the desire to go deeper in your walk with God, and you can close it a changed person. With every principle, promise, and truth, you'll find yourself living the Christian life fuller than before. Psalm 119:144 says, "The way you tell me to live is always right; help me understand it so I can live to the fullest" (Message).

Who wouldn't want to live this life to its fullest? And who couldn't use a peaceful renewing? I love how the Message phrases Psalm 119:114: "You're my place of quiet retreat; I wait for your Word to renew me."

Understand more about your heavenly Father by getting to know his heart through his Word. You can ask him this very minute to empower you, to give you the discipline and the yearning to grow closer to him through studying his Word. He longs to answer! Decide right now to let him become your place of quiet retreat and let his Word daily renew you.

I'm heading to that quiet retreat. Don't worry, I'll keep it a quiet retreat by making sure I don't wear the gong earrings.

I rejoice at Your word as one who finds great spoil. . . . Great peace have they who love Your law; nothing shall offend them or make them stumble. I am hoping and waiting [eagerly] for Your salvation, O Lord, and I do Your commandments. Your testimonies have I kept [hearing, receiving, loving, and obeying them]; I love them exceedingly! I have observed Your precepts and Your testimonies, for all my ways are [fully known] before You. . . . My lips shall pour forth praise [with thanksgiving and renewed trust] when You teach me Your statutes. My tongue shall [sing praise for the fulfillment] of Your word, for all Your commandments are righteous.

Psalm 119:162, 165–68, 171–72 AMP

Ruby-rooter 2

Believing Lies Is a Peace Blocker

I do love adding sparkle. Isn't accessorizing fun at about every turn? Accessorizing an outfit, sure, but I like adding that sparkly pizzazz to my car too (my rearview mirror is merely a holder for a shiny bauble). The shade on my desk lamp has cute dangly shinies suspended around its entire circumference. I think it shines a little brighter when it thinks it has its own necklace.

Even food is better with a little embellishment. I'm not just talking about a garnish of parsley here and a cupcake sprinkle there. Those are great, but I like to further accessorize my diet as a whole with a plateful of colorful vitamins every day.

I think I take about nine or ten vitamins each morning. I'm pretty sure I've got the entire vitamin and mineral alphabet covered. And I love how multicolored multivitamins tend to satisfy some of the guilt from the previous day's eating indiscretions. Down a load of vitamins and it undoes every Ding Dong and every bag of potato chips from the day before, right? I've even almost convinced myself a couple of times that if I take enough vitamins I'm going to look like one of the American Gladiators. At least a little Barbie-esque. Now that's embellishment.

Internal Combustion

One morning as I sorted through the papers, toys, and clutter on the kitchen counter and dutifully popped my handful of vitamins, I took a huge gulp of milk (skim milk, of course—to offset the Ding Dong). I was surprised when the vitamins went down a little rough. Which vitamin had the *prongs*?

That's when a little touch of panic tingled the back of my neck. *Hey, didn't I leave my earrings on the counter? Wait, did I leave them beside the vitamins? Oh my goodness, is that a cubic zirconium I feel working its way down my esophagus?* I was definitely feeling some friction. If I'd chased the vitamins with a little kindling, I don't doubt for a second that I could've started a fire.

Now there was an accessory turn I didn't see coming. Cubic-zirconium-initiated internal combustion.

Images of muffled laughter from ER people and X-ray technicians sent me into a higher state of panic. Accessorizing is fun, but from the inside? Not so much.

This Is Not All That Hard to Swallow

Physically, accessorizing on the inside can no doubt be painful. But spiritually speaking, accessorizing with truth on the inside never induces pain or panic. Exactly the opposite. It brings peace. It does remind us we need to be careful what we swallow. People who believe anything and everything are people who struggle with confusion—big panic, no peace. Keeping our minds on whatever is true means not swallowing lies.

There are so many troublesome lies bouncing around our culture today. And I'm sad to say, there are many women—even Christian women—who are swallowing those lies hook, line, and zirconium.

There's a peace-blocking lie, for instance, that says if you want to be loved and if you want to be happy, you have to look like an American Gladiator or a Barbie. What a crock. Don't believe that lie. Don't swallow even the smallest part of it. Your happiness has absolutely nothing to do with your looks. There are thousands of stunningly beautiful, yet tragically miserable women. And there are plainer women who shine with a joy that beats any billion-dollar gem. It's not about what we do with our looks. It's about what we do with Jesus.

Women are also swallowing the lie that this life is all about being happy and finding fulfillment. Not true. If our lives are wrapped up in and focused on anything other than Christ, on knowing him more and following him unswervingly, then we're setting ourselves up for some multipronged pain. Even though a life spent searching for happiness and fulfillment can lead to emptiness, the amazing truth is that as we focus on whatever is true and as we surrender to the purpose for which we've been created, that's when we find true happiness and fulfillment—even if we weren't looking for it! I love the way our God works!

Don't allow yourself to be sucked in by any of those other sneaky lies either, like those aimed at convincing you that you have no value. Those are lies that can trap you in sadness and fruitlessness. On the other hand, you can experience the most amazing peace as you fully know and understand the truth about who you are—and whose you are. Knowing you belong to the Lord who loves you gives you deeper understanding of your purpose in life and satisfies in a way nothing else can.

Consuming the Truth

Have you let any of these lies or other lies pull you down? Instead of swallowing lies that lead to every kind of insecurity, we need to consume God's truth. If your mind is all too often consumed with negative thoughts about yourself, your insides, or your outsides, spend some time dwelling on the truth—the truth of what God thinks of you. Spend time reading Psalm 139 and dwelling on how he so lovingly created you. He planned you in careful detail. He's thinking about you. He has a purpose for you. What wonderful truths! Consume them!

Consuming the truth and being careful not to swallow lies brings such sweet relief from the insecure life.

On a lighter note, you might be relieved to know that it wasn't my earring I swallowed. Turns out those earrings were on my dresser the whole time. I did notice, however, that there was a Barbie shoe missing.

And I never found it.

> O LORD, you have searched me
> and you know me.
> You know when I sit and when I rise;
> you perceive my thoughts from afar.
> You discern my going out and my lying down;
> you are familiar with all my ways.
> Before a word is on my tongue
> you know it completely, O LORD.
> You hem me in—behind and before;
> you have laid your hand upon me.
> Such knowledge is too wonderful for me,
> too lofty for me to attain.
> Where can I go from your Spirit?
> Where can I flee from your presence?
> If I go up to the heavens, you are there;
> if I make my bed in the depths, you are there.
> If I rise on the wings of the dawn,
> if I settle on the far side of the sea,

even there your hand will guide me,
　　your right hand will hold me fast. . . .
For you created my inmost being;
　　you knit me together in my mother's womb.
I praise you because I am fearfully and wonderfully made;
　　your works are wonderful,
　　I know that full well.
My frame was not hidden from you
　　when I was made in the secret place.
　　When I was woven together in the depths of the earth,
your eyes saw my unformed body.
　　All the days ordained for me
　　were written in your book
　　before one of them came to be.

Psalm 139:1–10, 13–16

CHA-CHING BLING　3

Quiet Time—the Why's

Don't get me wrong. I can appreciate a fine gem. I mean, there's jewelry and then there's jewelry. I think you'll understand what I mean when I tell you that 99.9 percent of my accessories fall into the first category. My "gems" are never quite as shiny as the blue light that was once flashing over them. Genuine? Of course. But genuine *what*? That's another question altogether.

So far none of my jewelry has kept any of my kids out of college. No piece in my collection has ever been more expensive than a new vehicle (and may I add that any jewel more expensive than my car had better be air conditioned and ready to transport me safely and comfortably to and from the mall).

I can give you some tips regarding the lower-cost bling. For instance, I've learned if the faux jewelry starts to turn, it's better not to mess with it. I dropped one of my rings in a good jewelry solvent and the entire thing disappeared. All I had left to remember the ring by was the green circle around my finger.

Even better than cleaning tips, how about some good reasons to appreciate the non-genuine jewels? Here are my top ten faves.

Top Ten Reasons It's a Relief to Have Inexpensive Jewelry

1. Most of your "gold" jewelry will float right to the surface if it accidentally slips off in the pool.
2. Your friends never desert you over jewel envy.
3. Instead of a big insurance policy, you can protect most of your jewelry with a really good rust inhibitor.
4. You can size the rings yourself with just a couple of squeezes.
5. Any thief who might break into your jewelry box would never get away with his felony since the uproarious laughter would immediately give him away.
6. Instead of one small gem at a time, you can buy most of your jewelry by the gross.
7. That favorite necklace might actually protect you from aberrant radiation.
8. When your favorite pieces start looking a little worn, a light coat of spray paint can shine them right back up.
9. This year's gold pieces can become next year's bronze pieces.
10. It's educational—since your kids can still go to college.

Sometimes it really is a relief to own a boxful of the not-so-genuine stuff. It's pretty telltale that if we had a fire at my house, even though I love my accessories, my jewelry box is about the last thing I would grab. I think in order of importance, it would be somewhere behind the coffeemaker, but just before that box of Ding Dongs in the pantry. Wait a minute. Chocolate. Okay, maybe just after the Ding Dongs.

How do you spell relief? F-A-C-T-O-R-Y M-A-D-E. There's something rather de-stressing about knowing your kiln-fired, lab-manufactured, chemically enhanced pieces are not such a huge investment that you'd need to go all out financially to replace them.

Smart Investing

Go either way in investing in your bling, but when it comes to investing time with your heavenly Father, there's only one way to go. All in. It's an investment in the health and success of your spirit. And it's much too important to neglect.

Wouldn't it be nice if we could read something one time and, *boom*, it was locked into our brain cells and into our lives forever? My brain cells are doing well to remember those Ding Dongs in the pantry. We need refreshers every day in those things that count. Reading God's Word is not only about the memorization of words and facts, but it's the ingraining of the principles and instructions into our beliefs, our thought patterns, our actions, our everyday way of life. If we want the Holy Spirit to inhabit and affect our everyday lives, then we need to come to him on an everyday basis.

Everyday Growth, Everyday Quiet Time

We do need a quiet time with the Father every day. Remember, as we spend time with him, we become more like him. He changes us.

As you were reading through the end of chapter one, did you actually ask him to empower you, discipline you, and give you the yearning to grow closer to him through studying his Word? Did you make an active decision to let him become that place of quiet retreat and to let his Word renew you every day? If so, this may be where that decision blossoms into a lifelong amazing change for you. Putting muscle to that decision and starting or building on your personal quiet time with him truly can bring you joy and peace in ways you never imagined. It can revolutionize your life.

So let's look at how to get to the "revolution" through these next two chapters. How do we approach this time with him and what does a quiet time involve? Our quiet time is focused, uninterrupted time spent in prayer and in reading and meditating on his Word. It's time just for him.

We Interrupt This Program for . . . a Message

Don't think I don't understand how challenging it can be to find a speck of time in the day that can be set apart as uninterruptable, much less quiet. Plans, preps, and programs—these schedules are bu-*sy!* It wasn't so long ago that I had a newborn, a two-year-old, a three-year-old, a five-year-old, and a seven-year-old. "Quiet" time became a relative term. That means my little relatives were hardly ever quiet. I had to get creative.

You may have to get creative too. Even sacrificial. You may have to sacrifice something from the schedule. Or you may have to sacrifice sleep every now and then to grab that quiet moment with your heavenly Father. But I can guarantee you they will be worthwhile sacrifices. You won't regret a second. He has a message for you. And the message he has for you can equip you to balance your daily chaos.

That's a good reason to plan your quiet time in the morning if at all possible. Not only is it like giving him your first time-fruits, so to speak, but it's also absolutely amazing how many times the Lord will give you some tidbit of wisdom or encouragement in your early morning quiet time that just fits a need you'll experience later in the day.

Read the Instructions First

I put together an ottoman a few weeks ago. I was pretty proud of myself, I must say. I'm not a handywoman, but for this project, I had to use a hammer—and even the drill. I'm never very brave when it comes to using power tools, but the whole procedure left me feeling pretty powerful. The ottoman came in a flat box full of a gajillion little pieces, and I got to watch as it sort of bloomed into a nifty footstool, piece by piece.

How silly would it have been for me to wrestle all day with those gajillion pieces, finally put them all together the best I could, and when the work was all finished, pull out the assembly instructions and *then* give them a thorough read? I might've accidentally built something that looked more like a chicken coop than a footstool.

If we read the instructions at the start, it's amazing how much more easily those pieces of our lives will fit together too. No need to be chicken in any situation when we're relying on God's Word—the ultimate power tool. Through his instructions, he can give us courage, training, security, happiness—spiritual wealth! Psalm 119:14 says, "Obeying your instructions brings as much happiness as being rich" (CEV). God's instructions. First.

Don't Let the Enemy Pull the Power Plug

Incidentally, when you're revving up for a power start, the Enemy will likely throw up every distraction he can. The last thing he wants is for you to experience a day powered by God the Father. He'll bring to mind everything you need to do for the day, and how you can't possibly squeeze in time for reading your Bible and praying to your Father. He'll try to convince you that your time would be better spent making a to-do list or taking care of those couple of chores. Have you ever been praying when thoughts of that load of laundry suddenly sprang to your mind? Or maybe an urgency about those papers you should've filed away?

I'm not sure how much of that is devil-influenced and how much is actually our own weak flesh, but I do believe there are battles of the mind that must be won in the name of the God of our quiet time. And I truly have no doubt that the Enemy is ready with a thousand distractions. He will slyly suggest that you need another hour of sleep much more than you need that time in Bible study and prayer. Don't listen. God's Word tells us Satan's a liar and the Father of Lies. He doesn't want to see a child of God empowered to live a day of victory and to experience God-given peace.

If you've been experiencing a lack of peace and power in your life, try plugging in to a discipline of Bible study and prayer. Invest your time and energies and get ready to experience some life-shaking power. It's eternally valuable. And still costs less than any jewelry— even the kind you have to break out of a plastic bubble.

> Praise be to you, O LORD;
>> teach me your decrees.
> With my lips I recount
>> all the laws that come from your mouth.
> I rejoice in following your statutes
>> as one rejoices in great riches.
> I meditate on your precepts
>> and consider your ways.
> I delight in your decrees;
>> I will not neglect your word.
>
> Psalm 119:12–16

---

4   MAGNUM OPAL

Quiet Time—the How's

Okay, who's making the weird noises? I was used to asking the question at home. After all, I have a houseful of teenagers. But I was at a women's conference. And I was the speaker! I didn't ask the question out loud, but I was scouring the crowd as I went on with my talk. I heard another muffled knock. Then a tinkly rattle. Then the knock again. How rude.

Several minutes into my talk, it finally occurred to me, much to my chagrin, that the rude person doing the knock-rattling . . . was *me*. I had clearly made a significant accessory misjudgment. Several in fact. The knock was the worst. Almost every time I moved, my dangly necklace swooshed into the lapel mic with that annoying thud. The rattle? My bracelet with the cute dangling opals. Who knew I was my own concerto? Of course, I might've figured it out sooner if my oversized earrings hadn't been jingling in my ears.

Necklace drumming into the mic, bracelet rattling around my wrist, earrings jingling in my ears—if I'd added cymbals to my knees and acquired a trained monkey, I could've been a decent street act.

Percussion Discussion

The accessories were cute, alright—coordinated perfectly with my outfit too. But I still had to reel them in and "lay them on the altar," as it were. I explained and confessed my unintentional percussion commotion to the audience, peeled off the jewelry, and piled it all on the corner of the podium. It looked like a little mound of treasure. I finished the talk bling-naked, but less distracted. I may have even started a new trend in jewelry with a beat. And I do love being trendy. I guess all's well that trends well.

The best trends, of course, are the ones that not only have a percussion beat you can tap your foot to, but repercussions you can build your life on. Percussions and *re*-percussions. The best trends are undoubtedly worth repeating.

That's why in the last chapter we looked at having a quiet time regularly—without missing a beat. We've looked at some why-to's. Let's talk about a few practical how-to's.

Even though we want to build a quiet time into our schedule without missing a beat, sometimes we need to dwell on the "quiet" aspect—all clanging accessories aside.

The "Quiet" of the Time

For some, there's not so much a struggle to find and keep a quiet time as there is to learn to embrace a little quiet in and of itself. Is hubbub such a big part of your life that you feel awkward the second there's no noise in the room? Does the quiet compel you to reach for the TV remote or turn on a radio?

In Psalm 46:10, the Lord tells us to "be still, and know that I am God." It's his desire that we quiet down and focus on him and him alone. Don't be afraid to start your quiet time with some genuine silence. Recognize his presence. Welcome him into your day.

You might be surprised what you find in that quiet place . . . what you discover about your holy God . . . what you discover about yourself . . . what you discover about your calling. Listen. Be ready to respond. Let there be quiet. Wait for him. Find yourself delighting in simply being with him and resting in him. Fill your mind and your soul with him.

If your mind starts to wander, reel those thoughts back in and learn to discipline your thinking. Retraining those thought patterns might take awhile. That's okay. Just because those thoughts have had brain-reign for a long time doesn't mean you can't learn a new way of quiet, peace-filled thinking. As you embrace his quiet, you can find yourself in true worship. It's the kind of worship that brings peace to even the noisiest brain and peace to even the most flustered heart.

Still having trouble getting past the "quiet" dynamic? Ask the Lord himself to help you. He will answer. Zephaniah 3:17 says, "The LORD your God is with you, he is mighty to save. He will take great delight in you, he will quiet you with his love." He desires that special, close time with you and if you ask him, he can lovingly quiet you.

Details, Details

We women love details. So how about a few detailed suggestions to think about as you approach your quiet time. "REV UP"—get ready for your time with him.

Reach out to him expectantly. Come expecting. He loves you and delights in time with you. And he is all-powerful. No real encounter with the all-powerful God of the universe will leave you untouched, unchanged. Expect something radical. Expect a blessing. Then hold on to your hats, sisters, because he delivers!

Endeavor to seek him and him alone. It's easy to get into a wrong way of thinking, supposing your quiet time is really all about you. But selfish seeking is not worship. It's not about what's in it for you. It's easy to seek a blessing or to seek an experience. Instead, seek him and him alone and those other things will often follow anyway. "Seek the LORD your God, and you will find Him if you seek Him with all your heart and with all your soul" (Deut. 4:29 NKJV).

View the map. Read the Bible. "Hear" what he has to say to you through his Word. Commentaries and devotionals and study helps are great—other tools are helpful as well, but don't let them replace his Word. Don't study the studies as much as you study his Word. Read through a few verses, a few chapters, or an assigned portion of Scripture from a particular study or guide. Let your Father communicate his truth to you.

Use it UP. Apply what you've read in the most God-ward direction by asking yourself some questions:

Is there . . .

- a command to obey?
- a sin to confess?
- a sin to avoid?
- a truth to learn?
- a principle to employ?

- a promise to claim?
- a praise to offer?
- a service to consider?

Pray. Pray through the answers to the "use it UP" questions. In the next chapter, we'll look at some more of the particulars that can help you in the prayer part of your quiet time. Peruse those before you pray or even during prayer and let them spark even more sweet time of communion with your heavenly Father.

Prayer and reading God's Word are essential for leading a life filled with the peace of God. As a matter of fact, if we tried to give the Bible a subtitle, it might just be "How to Find Real Peace." Peace is an underlying subtheme of so much of what we see in Scripture, from beginning to end. There was peace in the Garden of Eden until Adam and Eve's sin threw in a peace-demolishing monkey wrench. There is peace fulfilled through Christ by his sacrificial death on the cross to purchase our salvation, our peace with God. There is peace for living available to every person who trusts in the Lord and walks in his Spirit. And there is the anticipation of an eternal kingdom where Christ rules and there is a sinless, delicious, perfect peace for all eternity.

Let the Lord use your time in his Word and your prayer time to kindle more and more peace. Your quiet time can bring such amazing, blazing treasure into your life. Not the pile-it-on-the-podium kind of treasure. No, this is heart treasure. And it can radically revolutionize your walk with Christ.

Go ahead. Be radical. Your friends may tell you that spending time every day in Bible study and prayer is a little fanatical. Don't buy it. March to the beat of a different drummer.

Or knee cymbals. Whichever.

> Let my cry come right into your presence, God;
> > provide me with the insight that comes only from your
> > Word.
> Give my request your personal attention,
> > rescue me on the terms of your promise.

Let praise cascade off my lips;
    after all, you've taught me the truth about life!
And let your promises ring from my tongue;
    every order you've given is right.
Put your hand out and steady me
    since I've chosen to live by your counsel.
I'm homesick, God, for your salvation;
    I love it when you show yourself!
Invigorate my soul so I can praise you well,
    use your decrees to put iron in my soul.
And should I wander off like a lost sheep—seek me!
    I'll recognize the sound of your voice.

Psalm 119:169–76 Message

SUPPLEMENTATION OF 5
ORNAMENTATION

Quiet Time—Prayer

I do love a sparkle-heavy event—any excuse to bring on the bling!
I enthusiastically embrace every opportunity to dress to the nines.
And being one who so often likes to take the bling to the next ridiculous level, I've been known to even shoot for the tens. Hasn't it been said that "anything worth doing is worth excessively overdoing"? Wait. Now that I think about it, maybe I was the one who said that.

In that vein, I found what I was sure would be the perfect glam-jacket for any froufrou event. It had the most wonderfully wild, shiny vertical trim down the front edge from collar to hem. I couldn't wait for a fancy enough occasion to take it for a test run.

But when that occasion finally arrived, I had a bit of a shock. I caught a glimpse of myself in the ladies' room mirror and saw the jacket in a whole new light. *What in the world?* In that lighting, the trim on the jacket looked more like a *landing strip*.

Fashion Runway or Airport Runway?

An outfit embellished with runway lights was not my idea of high fashion. It's hard to enjoy a fancy event when you have to spend so much of the evening worrying about stray planes touching down across your middle.

Next time I'm on a glam hunt, I'm definitely shopping more carefully. I'm simply not sure the over-the-top sparkles were stunning enough to warrant dealing all night with garb that that would attract airport operators and their signal flashlights.

To further complicate the bling situation, the jacket was spewing sprinkles. Everywhere I went I left little pools of sparkles. I was getting worried. As over-the-top as the jacket turned out to be, I still couldn't begin to picture what it would look like with all its sparkles gone. At the rate it was losing the sprinkles, I was afraid the jacket would be naked by midnight. Yikes.

Why Did the Lady Cross the Road?

It was a bit of a relief to find out I wasn't the only one at the event with a garment that was decomposing. One lady was losing feathers left and right. I thought for a minute she was molting. When she left the room, several people looked at her chair and deduced she must've been sitting on a chicken the whole time. Which came first, the chicken or the chair? Another woman left a sequin trail so clear that we could've tracked her all the way home.

Wouldn't it be nice if the hosts and hostesses of formal events set up an "ornamentation restoration station"—some sort of "frock shop" to make needed bling repairs? Losing glitter? They could haul you up on a rack and spray on another coat. Feathers flying away? A few quill extensions and you'd be as good as new. What a relief it would be to have some supplemental bling available for any breach in ornamentation.

Then again, some might argue that I put the "mental" in supplemental.

Not Just Supplemental—This Is Monumental

Prayer is entirely different. It's not just supplemental. It's fundamental. And in keeping our minds on whatever is true, it's instrumental. We must keep our minds surrounded by, focused on, bathed in, and infused by prayer.

We're instructed to "pray without ceasing" (1 Thess. 5:17), yes, but in addition to keeping our hearts and minds in an attitude of prayer, regular, purposeful, set-apart prayer times need to have a central place in our mentality and our schedule. The previous chapter gave suggested quiet time points to help compose a concert of Bible study and prayer. If your quiet time is a symphony, prayer is like its grand finale.

Need a little help knowing where to begin? Just in case, you can always BEGIN here:

Bow before the greatness of your glorious heavenly Father. He deserves your worship. Bow heart, soul, mind—everything you are and everything you have—in worship, praise, and thanks. Adore him, praise him for his greatness, and thank him for the blessings he's given you. When you bow before him in loving worship, you're doing exactly what you were built to do. Nothing could be sweeter. This is the time to take your eyes off of self and place your focus completely on him.

Examine your life. As we worship him in his holiness, our own unholiness becomes clearer than the most blinding sparkle-dress. Ask him to show you your sin. Own up to it, confess and forsake that sin. Some people put off having a quiet time because they feel uneasy when it comes to prayer. Just as Adam didn't want to face God in the Garden of Eden after he sinned, we find it anything but comfortable facing our holy God when there's sin we've let slide. We need to draw on 1 John 1:9 every day: "But if we confess our sins to him, he is faithful and just to forgive us and to cleanse us from every wrong" (NLT[a]). Get rid of that sin and embrace his glorious forgiveness.

Go through a passage of Scripture, praying through his Word. When we're praying his Word back to him, we know we're praying in his will. It's powerful! Pray through the application questions listed in the previous chapter. Ask the Lord to use his Word to make you more and more the servant he wants you to be. Surrender to whatever he wants to do in your life.

Intercede. Pray for the needs of your family, your friends, your church, and your government. Your heavenly Father cares about every detail of life. Pray about your own needs as well. We never want our prayer time to become a to-do list we simply hand over to the Lord. But that doesn't mean we don't ask. As a matter of fact, he's instructed us to ask, and when we don't, we miss out. James 4:2 says, "You do not have, because you do not ask God," and Luke 18:7 tells us "God will always give what is right to his people who cry to him night and day" (NCV).

Nourish your spirit. Singing songs to the Lord or listening to praise music can keep your mind pointed God-ward. Many people like to sort of reinforce their quiet time with recording praises, prayer requests, thoughts about the day's Scripture reading, and so forth, in a journal or notebook. It's wonderfully faith-building to see the Lord answer your prayers and to be able to make those blessed checkmarks beside the prayer needs you've listed.

Every Morning, BEGIN Again

We have a new opportunity every day to come before our God. Would you like to sense your Father tapping on the door of your heart like never before? Would you like to see him fill you with power and use you in amazing and marvelous ways? Prayer is the answer to the tapping and the power for the service.

Do you desperately want to see the Lord move in your life, yet you find you're rarely kneeling before him in intimate times of prayer? He wants to work in your life. He longs to see you enjoying a tender intimacy with him, to take you into a new place of loving fellowship with himself—satisfied and at peace. But that won't happen if you're not drawing close to him in prayer. There is such peace and power in that place of closeness with him! Romans 12:12 tells us to be "faithful in prayer."

Incidentally, when things aren't going well or you're frustrated with life, don't think that means you need to skip your prayer time. Just the opposite. That's the perfect time for a fresh touch from him. Be open and honest about how you're feeling. You can't tell him anything he doesn't already know—he knows it all.

Through it all, tell him that your heart's desire is to obey. As you do, you'll find new heights in prayer and new depths of peace. It's at that point of complete surrender—emptying yourself and giving him everything—that you suddenly find you have absolutely everything you've ever needed. You'll love finding his peace surrounding and encircling your life.

And it forever beats planes circling a glitter-spangled jacket.

When you pray, you should go into your room and close the door and pray to your Father who cannot be seen. Your Father can see what is done in secret, and he will reward you.

And when you pray, don't be like those people who don't know God. They continue saying things that mean nothing, thinking that God will hear them because of their many words. Don't be like them, because your Father knows the things you need before you ask him. So when you pray, you should pray like this:

> "Our Father in heaven,
> may your name always be kept holy.
> May your kingdom come

and what you want be done,
    here on earth as it is in heaven.
Give us the food we need for each day.
Forgive us for our sins,
    just as we have forgiven those who sinned against us.
And do not cause us to be tempted,
but save us from the Evil One."
[The kingdom, the power, and the glory are yours forever.
    Amen.]

Matthew 6:6–13 NCV

PART 2

"KEEP YOUR MINDS ON WHATEVER IS . . . PURE"

As the Ring Turns 6

Guard against Emotion-Centered Life

I'm not a fan of soap operas, I'll just tell you right up front. What a waste of emotions. If I had to come up with a soap, though, I think I would go with a title something like *Clichés of Our Lives*—or maybe *One Life to Waste*.

How about *The Young and the Witless*? Or wait, even better, how about an accessory-themed soap: *As the Ring Turns*, a soap opera about fake metals that start out one color and end up another. It's an emotional upheaval just waiting to happen.

Taking a Bad Turn

Have you ever had a cheap ring that turned faster than a ripe banana? One metal tone when you bought it, totally new look a couple of months later? It's like a mood ring except that it's not only the stone that changes color—and you're usually not in the mood.

It once happened to a favorite bracelet of mine. I pulled it out to wear one morning and found that the gold bracelet I had so enjoyed wearing was not what it used to be. Gold tone? Not anymore. It was brownish with leprosy-looking bronzy splotches.

Okay, it was definitely not a high-end bracelet to begin with, but talk about taking a turn for the worse. I could string Cocoa Puffs together and get about the same look as the bracelet. Granted, I'm sure it would've stayed crunchy even in milk, but I had a bit of an emotional attachment to that piece of jewelry. It's sad when a good bracelet goes bad. Picture the back of my hand on my forehead. Oh the melodrama.

Emotional Attachments

It's often surprising how easy it is to let our emotions get the better of us. Sometimes we not only let them get the better of us but actually let them rule our lives. We don't always associate the effect our emotions have on our thinking and our actions, but they're as closely tied together as the morphing of my gold-tone bracelet into my splotchy bronze one. Overemotional thinking results in out-of-control emotional responses. Once you're on that ride, strap yourself in—it's going to be rough. Who needs the roller-coaster life?

If we want to keep our minds on whatever is pure, we need to rein in those emotions and rein in our thinking. The Greek word for what we read as "don't ever stop thinking" later in this passage is the word *logizomai*. It's a word that refers to settling your mind so that the object of your thoughts affects your conduct, influencing and changing the way you behave. If we *logizomai* emotional, feeling-based thoughts, guess what we'll see fleshed out in our behavior?

If You Don't Mind . . .

Never think for a moment that what goes on in your mind is not important. Just because your thoughts are invisible to you doesn't mean they're invisible to God. And it certainly doesn't mean they have no effect. Your thoughts shape your actions. Proverbs 23:7 says, "For as he thinks within himself, so he is" (NASB), and Proverbs 4:23 says, "Be careful what you think, because your thoughts run your life" (NCV). Your thoughts determine whether you live in fear, bitterness, negativity, and the like, or live in the peace of God. Did you know that it's your thoughts that determine your level of peace, and not your circumstances?

"Keep your minds on whatever is . . . pure"

In his book *A Love Worth Giving*, Max Lucado said, "Change the thoughts, and you change the person. If today's thoughts are tomorrow's actions, what happens when we fill our minds with thoughts of God's love? . . . It's not enough to keep the bad stuff out. We've got to let the good stuff in. . . . 'Thinking' [in Philippians 4:8] conveys the idea of pondering—studying and focusing, allowing what is viewed to have an impact on us."[1]

Come, Let Us Get Emotional Together?

We can let God's Word and his peace have an impact on us, or we can let our wishy-washy, up-and-down emotions rule us. An emotion-ruled life is a soap opera life full of messes to clean up and plenty of confusion. It's like basing life decisions on the color of a mood ring. Color us all confused!

In Isaiah 1:18 it's the Lord himself who says, "Come, let us reason together." No need to check reason at the door. We women can sometimes use our emotions as an excuse for tossing reason out the window and responding however we want. But surrendering to our emotions is not the way to think pure thoughts or live a pure life. You are not a victim of your thoughts. You have a choice of what you will or will not dwell on. I think that's why Paul spends so much energy in Scripture sounding the charge to choose our thoughts well.

Please Keep Arms and Hands Inside His Peace

Feelings-based living will lead us on that roller-coaster ride in the wrong direction. Don't get on that ride. Let the right and pure thinking that comes through focusing on the right things set the pattern for living—the pattern for living that will lead you down the track of peace.

In Colossians 3:2 we're called to think in the right direction: "Set your minds on things above, not on earthly things." Those "things above" are the things of Christ.

The earthly things? I think they're more like those things that may be part of a complete and balanced breakfast, but you still wouldn't want to wear them to a nice dinner party.

> Since you have been raised to new life with Christ, set your sights on the realities of heaven, where Christ sits in the place of honor at God's right hand. Think about the things of heaven, not the things of earth. For you died to this life, and your real life is hidden with Christ in God. And when Christ, who is your life, is revealed to the whole world, you will share in all his glory.
>
> So put to death the sinful, earthly things lurking within you. Have nothing to do with sexual immorality, impurity, lust, and evil desires. Don't be greedy, for a greedy person is an idolater, worshiping the things of this world. Because of these sins, the anger of God is coming. You used to do these things when your life was still part of this world. But now is the time to get rid of anger, rage, malicious behavior, slander, and dirty language. Don't lie to each other, for you have stripped off your old sinful nature and all its wicked deeds. Put on your new nature, and be renewed as you learn to know your Creator and become like him.
>
> Colossians 3:1–10 NLT[b]

7   BLING RADAR

Getting Rid of Sin, Living Honorably

At my house, we're all a bunch of losers.

I don't mean that in the normal sense of the loser label. I'm convinced that all the members of my family are striving to be honorable people. But I have to tell you, every one of us is a total loser at least once a week when it comes to misplacing things.

I lost a pair of my favorite earrings a couple of months ago, then last week found them again after all that time (they were in the bottom of my purse—no wonder I couldn't find them), only to lose them again the next day. Where's bling radar when you need it?

We're not just jewelry losers. Tennis racquet, keys, glasses, purse, baseball uniform, cell phone, retainer, wallet, book bag, tennis shoes—you name it, we've lost it.

Remote Location

We were searching for the lost TV remote recently. Again. We looked in the sofa, under the chair, behind the end table . . . inside the DVD player. We looked everywhere but still hadn't even a "remote" idea where it was.

Every time we plan to watch something on TV at my house, we have to build in an extra half hour for the remote search. Show starts at 8:00 Central? If we don't want to miss the first half, we have to start the hunt in Mountain Time. If the kids had the remote last, it's likely closer to Pacific.

The TV remote doesn't have one of those pager buttons like the cordless phone. Why ever not? Or why can't the remote simply sense that it's ten feet or more from the TV, sprout some little mechanical legs, and maneuver its way back toward the sofa? With little claws, it might even be able to crawl out from the depths of the chair cushion.

Or maybe we could at least push some sort of pager that would make it send out little puffs of smoke. Yeah, smoke signals. That could work.

Of course, I guess we could use all the energy we spend searching for the remote to simply walk over to the TV and push the buttons on the set. No, that would be weird. It's just not our way. And you can't flick through thirty channels per second. Isn't it strange, though, that sometimes we'll take apart the DVD player instead of just getting up and pushing the buttons? Misdirected energies?

Are You Pondering What I'm Pondering?

Misdirection happens on the spiritual side when we stop looking to the Lord for true direction. It's something to think about. In fact, the psalmist thought about it in Psalm 119:59: "I pondered the direction of my life, and I turned to follow your laws" (NLT[b]). We learn there that when we see our lives headed in the wrong direction, we need to think about it, yes. But it doesn't stop there. It's not enough just to think about it. We need to turn. Turn and follow the Lord through his Word. Verse 64 says, "O LORD, your unfailing love fills the earth; teach me your decrees" (NLT[b]).

If we want to live the pure life we're called to "think on" and "do" in our focal passage in Philippians, we need to understand that the only right direction is his direction. I love it that Psalm 119:64 reminds me that his direction is forever and always the direction of amazing, unfailing love.

His love inspires us to be pure, respectable, and honorable. The Greek word translated "pure" in Philippians 4:8 communicates the idea of just that: being worthy of respect, being forthright and honorable—just the opposite of sin.

Let Go of the Loser Life

Coming face-to-face with our own impurity is anything but pleasant. Talk about feeling like a total loser. It's not fun to admit you've been going the wrong direction.

When Adam and Eve sinned, everything changed for them—and for us too. It was the misdirection of all time. And when it happened, Adam's shame led him to hide from God.

In Genesis 3:9, "the LORD God called to Adam and said to him, 'Where are you?'" (NKJV). God didn't ask Adam the "where are you" question because he really didn't know where Adam was. He hadn't "misplaced" the joy of his creation. This was not your average game of hide-and-seek. God is omniscient. He simply couldn't "not know" where Adam was any more than Adam could actually hide from God.

So why did he ask? I think the Lord wanted Adam to ponder, to stop and think about where he was. He had been in perfect fellowship with God. To fall from that holy place to a place of disobedience and a life in a fallen world must've been almost more than he could comprehend. But God called him to think about it.

Ready to Rethink and Redirect?

God calls us to think about it too. We have to face the misdirection and lose the sin before we can take hold of the pure life. And do you know what is required to let go of the loser life and head in a right, pure direction? One step. One step is all it takes to stop being a loser and to embrace honor. It's a step of surrender. When we confess our sin and forsake it, we experience a new closeness to the Lord.

When he becomes your all, you can daily surrender every difficulty, every worry, every struggle—and it's there you find sweet peace. This is what God your Father wants for you! And have you ever thought about the fact that God wants more from you than a sinless life? He wants to be *with* you—to help you resist temptation, to give you power to say no to sin. He wants to share with you the peaceful, contented, honorable life.

Romans 6:6 says, "For we know that our old self was crucified with him so that the body of sin might be done away with, that we should no longer be slaves to sin." As we say good-bye to that dishonorable life as a slave to sin and understand his indwelling power to live well, we can finally have the ability to truly say no to sin. God wants to protect you from that hurtful sin. He wants to live with you every minute of the day and to love you all along the way.

Are you ready to embrace the pure and honorable life? Don't try it in your own strength. The only way to experience it is to let go of self and let go of the sin that will keep you at arm's length from a holy God. Name the sin. Ugly? Oh yes. Painful to admit? You bet. But as we ponder the ugliness of our sin and ask him to forgive, we can have the loving fellowship with the Father that will meet our every heart's desire. And we can walk with him the pure and honorable life.

And, hey, I'm not just blowing smoke.

So you also should consider yourselves to be dead to the power of sin and alive to God through Christ Jesus.
Do not let sin control the way you live; do not give in to sinful desires. Do not let any part of your body become an instrument of evil to serve sin. Instead, give yourselves completely to God, for you were dead, but now you have new life. So use your whole body as an instrument to do what is right for the glory of God. Sin is no longer your master, for you no longer live under the requirements of the law. Instead, you live under the freedom of God's grace.

Romans 6:11–14 NLT[b]

8 WHEN YOU'VE SEEN ONE ENCLOSED SHOPPING CENTER, YOU'VE SEEN A MALL

Sin Results in Loneliness

Accessorizing is not for wimps. It takes stamina. Fortitude. Gumption. A willingness to endure the hardship of standing alone. It even takes good neck muscles.

I was shopping at the mall with a couple of my boys. We were in the jewelry department in one of the bigger stores, and I was trying to decide between about a dozen "perfect" necklaces. To get the best side-by-side comparison view, I tried on the whole dozen at once.

"KEEP YOUR MINDS ON WHATEVER IS . . . PURE"

Daniel thought it was weird that no one else seemed to notice that his mom was having what looked like a psychotic accessory episode. He was ready to gather an intervention team. Or maybe take me to Mardi Gras.

Someone Needs a Makeover

I had to agree with him at least a little when I looked in the mirror and scared myself. I looked like the next project person on TLC's *What Not to Wear*. In my mind's eye I could see Stacy and Clinton rolling their eyes with a "What could she be thinking??" and maybe backing that up with a snide, "What? Fat Tuesday already?"

That's when I decided to hurry. But which one of the dozen "perfect" necklaces should I buy? Should I go ahead and get them all? That's when Daniel asked, "Are you thinking what I'm thinking?"

Bless the boy. I looked at the price tags and answered, "Were you thinking our family could give up eating for about a month and a half so I can get all of them? If so, then yes."

That was totally *not* what he was thinking. He was thinking about a strawberry-banana smoothie from Smoothie Palooza at the food court.

The boys were even less supportive when they found out I wanted to go to two more shopping places before heading home. Of course, guys don't understand the female shopping concept. We women know that to make sure you're getting the perfect item at the perfect price, you shop every store in three surrounding counties that might carry that item. To the guys, one store is about the same as another. I'm sure they figured that if you've seen one enclosed shopping center you've seen 'em all. Or seen a mall. Either way. And either way, all the boys wanted to do was get a smoothie and go home.

Move over, Maytag repairman. Proper accessorizing can be a lonely job.

It's a Lonely Job, but Somebody's Got to Do It

Loneliness can crop up in the most unexpected places sometimes. Are you feeling lonely? We'll talk about plugging in to people in chapters 21 through 25. But as strange as this might sound, sometimes loneliness is not a people-related thing. You can be surrounded by the most loving friends and family and still feel lonely. Sometimes it's all about our relationship with God. Impurity, sin, separates us from the Father and births an overwhelming soul-loneliness that puts peace far out of reach. No purity, no peace. Psalm 25:16–18 says, "Turn to me and have mercy on me, because I am lonely and hurting. My troubles have grown larger; free me from my problems. Look at my suffering and troubles, and take away all my sins" (NCV).

You have a heavenly Father who loves and treasures you and desires to be close to you. Considering his love and his desire to be close, it hardly seems possible that we could experience loneliness, does it? But loneliness happens in the biggest way when we're separated from the Father because of sin we're clutching. Clutching that sin is letting go of the Father and letting go of that sense of peace-giving fellowship and communion with him. Every time we choose our own way instead of his way, we're breaking our close companionship with him.

How do we fix the loneliness? Confession. As soon as sin is confessed, intimacy is restored with the Lord. What a relief it is to regain our peace and to experience his presence again! It's like a party. So much better than Mardi Gras.

Pay No Attention to That Sin Behind the Curtain

Ignore it and it'll go away? That's not the way it works with sin. There's no magic formula for making life better. No heel clicking can fix it. If we refuse to forsake sin, the separation widens and the loneliness deepens.

Are you aching to have freedom from sin and a renewed harmony with your heavenly Father? Are you just dying to squelch the soul-loneliness and return again to the Promised Land of fellowship with God? The Israelites had to leave Egypt before they could step into that Promised Land. You can step into freedom and sweet fellowship too. Name the sin that's keeping you in the slavery of Egypt. Don't simply hint at it. Call it what it is: ugly. It's that ugliness that's zapping your peace and leaving you in frustrated loneliness.

Believe that your God can forgive you and that he can give you God-sized victory over sin. The Israelites took the long route to the Promised Land. They spent forty years circling the desert. Why? Their unbelief.

That Middle Eastern desert might've been a pretty lonely place—even with a few million of your closest friends and family making the trip with you. Take the shortest road to victory. Even if you've been struggling for a long time with a particular sin, believe that God can free you. Victory is yours because your God has the power.

Come On In for Some Milk and Honey

No need to stay stuck in the lonely life. Let the Lord know how much you hate your sin and how much you despise everything that keeps you separated from him and keeps you powerless and peace-less, stuck in painful loneliness. Ask the Father to take away anything and everything that separates you from him. Ask with everything you've got; pray it with every ounce of your heart's strength. He will answer! And when he does, that loneliness will be replaced with glorious celebration. It's a Promised Land party just waiting for you to enjoy with the Father who adores you tenderly and who seeks to share sweet fellowship with you. Milk and honey all around!

Hey, milk and honey. Isn't that the flavor of the month at Smoothie Palooza's?

> Blessed is he whose transgression is forgiven,
> Whose sin is covered.

Blessed is the man to whom the LORD does not impute
    iniquity,
    And in whose spirit there is no deceit.

When I kept silent, my bones grew old
    Through my groaning all the day long.
For day and night Your hand was heavy upon me;
    My vitality was turned into the drought of summer. Selah
I acknowledged my sin to You,
    And my iniquity I have not hidden.
    I said, "I will confess my transgressions to the LORD,"
    And You forgave the iniquity of my sin. Selah

Psalm 32:1–5 NKJV

9   BLING, BLING—HELLO?

No Peace with Guilt

It's one thing to see a kiosk at the mall filled with cell phones. But a kiosk at the mall filled with little *outfits* for cell phones? Now that's different. Maybe you're thinking about coordinating your new suit with a new suit for your cellie. It could happen. I wouldn't be surprised to find out that there are fashion magazines exclusively for phone-wear.

I'm expecting my cell phone to complain to me any day now about the fact that all the other phones have cool clothes and how my cell never gets to do anything. Maybe even how I "just don't understand." I have the nerve to keep slipping my phone in its plain, ol' black pouch. Oh, the cell fashion tragedy. If my phone could roll its eyes and flip its hair, I have no doubt it would.

    "KEEP YOUR MINDS ON WHATEVER IS . . . PURE"

Ring-a-Bling-Bling

Phones are not only ringing these days but blinging too. I recently saw a gal pull out a cell phone that was wearing more jewelry than I was. Yes, the phone, not the gal. Jeweled buttons, a fancy pink cover with a rhinestone strap, and a furry pink tassel—this cell was to phones what poodles are to dogs.

Phone fluff is not cheap either. I don't know about you, but if I'm going to spend that much money dressing a phone, I better have given birth to the thing. And it better need the new outfits for college—where it plans to get a degree, leading to a great job, after which it plans to support me in the manner to which I'd like to become accustomed.

I thought it was funny that even with all that fluff and frou on the lady's poodle-phone, would you believe it, the overembellished cell wouldn't work! The woman had forgotten to charge it. Isn't that a little ironic? The poor phone was all dressed up with no place to dial. What a total disconnect.

Can You Hear Me Now? Good

We looked at how impurity disconnects us from fellowship with God and disconnects us from the peace he gives. Every time we sin, it's like hanging up on the grace of God. But the instant we get rid of sin, understand the wrongness of it, and ask to be cleansed from the ugliness of it, the line is clear again. Connection restored. Hello, peace.

Trying to get rid of guilt yourself won't work, of course. People who try to get rid of their own guilt and guilt feelings usually end up giving up and simply trying to numb it all with booze or drugs or some other destructive practice. Or they may try to mask it with good deeds—less harmful, but still completely ineffective. There's only one way to get rid of guilt. Jesus. He took it for us on the cross. Why in the world would we try to take it back?

It's also just about as power-draining when we clog up the communication lines again by dredging up the old sin that he's already forgiven. Why would we bring it up again when God has separated us from its punishment as far as the east is from the west?

Hold the Phone

His sacrifice was enough. He died for that sin—it's been paid for once and for all. Don't underestimate the power of his grace—a grace that is infinitely bigger than you can sin. Asking for forgiveness and then refusing to accept it or failing to understand that it's yours is as unproductive as spiffing up a cell phone but then neglecting to charge it. Where's the power?

The Enemy doesn't want you living in that place of powerful connection, that place of clear communication with your Father. So if he can cause static by convincing you that your sin is inexcusable, he can render you fruitless. When you waste time and energy worrying over sin that Jesus has already taken care of, Satan has you where he wants you—too distracted by guilt to fulfill the purposes the Lord has called you to. The Enemy wins. You end up all dressed up with no fruit to bear. Guilt is the un-gift that keeps on un-giving.

When guilt keeps calling, hang up. Move on. Let that guilt know it has reached a number that has been disconnected or is no longer in service. You're again in the service of the Lord God!

Service Has Been Restored

Can you imagine what it must've been like for the disciples when Jesus appeared to them in that upper room after his crucifixion? They weren't yet convinced of the resurrection. They were defeated, full of fear—probably pretty pitiful, really. Everything they had poured their lives into for three years . . . gone. All hope for the future, every dream . . . crushed.

To top it all off, they likely knew they'd totally blown it. When push came to shove, most of them ran and hid. As a matter of fact, that's probably what they were doing in that room—hiding. When

"KEEP YOUR MINDS ON WHATEVER IS . . . PURE"

Jesus appeared to them, do you think they were expecting a lecture about how they had failed and a deposition about everything they should've done differently? I wonder if they were cringing, getting ready to be blasted with a stern speech, being asked why they were cowering and where their faith was. Jesus would've been completely justified in delivering that kind of speech. But what were his very first words to his defeated, trembling disciples? "Peace be with you." What did they lack? Peace. What did he offer? Peace.

> Then, the same day at evening, being the first day of the week, when the doors were shut where the disciples were assembled, for fear of the Jews, Jesus came and stood in the midst, and said to them, "Peace be with you." When He had said this, He showed them His hands and His side. Then the disciples were glad when they saw the Lord. So Jesus said to them again, "Peace to you! As the Father has sent Me, I also send you."
>
> John 20:19–21 NKJV

Long Distance? No Way!

Isn't it wonderful that Jesus doesn't measure out his peace and his love and his grace? He simply lavishes it. He doesn't dole it out to us according to our success. He doesn't take it back because we fail. He simply loves us. He desires a closeness with us.

You can draw near to your loving heavenly Father. Don't let guilt keep you from doing it. Hebrews 10:22 says, "Let us come near to God with a sincere heart and a sure faith, because we have been made free from a guilty conscience" (NCV).

Jesus offered peace to his disciples with a second peace greeting in verse 21 of John 20 when he said, "Peace to you!" And then he commissioned them. He let them know that he would be sending them out, using them to advance the kingdom of God. What an honor! And what a change—from a total lack of peace to a calling of peace and purpose. From powerless to supercharged. Receiving the forgiveness Jesus offers and the peace he gives gets us set to serve. Powered up and ready! Praise God! What an exciting occurrence it is to go from immobilized to geared up and ready for action!

Mobilized to serve. This kind of service mobilization, incidentally, is in no way related to your mobile service.

> And so, dear brothers and sisters, we can boldly enter heaven's Most Holy Place because of the blood of Jesus. By his death, Jesus opened a new and life-giving way through the curtain into the Most Holy Place. And since we have a great High Priest who rules over God's house, let us go right into the presence of God with sincere hearts fully trusting him. For our guilty consciences have been sprinkled with Christ's blood to make us clean, and our bodies have been washed with pure water.
>
> Let us hold tightly without wavering to the hope we affirm, for God can be trusted to keep his promise.
>
> Hebrews 10:19–23 NLT[b]

10 Buttons and Boas

Self-esteem vs. Others-esteem

I've noticed that there are lots of instances when accessories can inspire a better mood. I mean, really. Has there ever been a time you saw a feather boa on someone and not smiled? They're to die for! I must say, the perfect cute scarf can make you feel pretty good about yourself.

The frustrating part is that scarves are in style, then they're out. In. Out. In. Out. Who can keep up? Then again, does it really matter? I've seen scarves come and go, and I've finally decided that if I like it, I'm wearing it. Of course, it took a few years for me to come to that place of accessory maturity.

At least I have gained some tidbits of scarf insight along the way. I'm happy to share my acquired scarf knowledge—as well as some of the mysterious scarf unknowns—with you, my girlfriends.

Top 10 Bits of Scarf Wisdom I Have Learned

1. There are more ways to tie scarves than there are Boy Scout knots—and they're much more complicated. No one knows the reason.
2. The scarf you always liked will come back into style as soon as you sell it in your garage sale for a dime.
3. Catsup is attracted to a new scarf in direct proportion to how much you like the new scarf. No one knows the reason.
4. Old scarves never die . . . but with enough catsup spills, they can sure smell like they have.
5. People with long, fringed scarves should never stand over a wood chipper.
6. Scarves can be given as gifts for men, but not pink scarves with rhinestones. Most people know the reason.
7. No one should ever go on a safari without a scarf. It might be the only way out of random lion pits and surprise quicksand. It's also a tourniquet, makeshift mosquito net, and can make a good-looking turban to cover safari hair.
8. Scarves are useful in many other ways. MacGyver never used a pocketknife until he lost his scarf.
9. Women who are about to bend over a birthday cake to blow out their candles should first take off their scarves. One combustible scarf plus a perfume accelerant can equal no eyebrows for several months.
10. Women should never wear a scarf that looks like one of those flags that truckers tie on an oversized load. The reason should be obvious.

A correctly tied scarf is a thing of beauty. Art almost. It's like . . . scarf-i-gami. I get a warm feeling just thinking about it. As a matter of fact, scarves are good for a warm feeling all the way around. Wearing a scarf in the winter is about more than good looks. It's like a little coat for your neck. Think about it!

Me, My Scarf, and I

Think about this too. To experience consistent peace, we're called to consistently think about things that are pure. We're called to think about what we're thinking about, as it were. So what about thinking about myself? What about ME? Where do thoughts of self fit in?

Society has made such a huge point in recent years to hammer home the "you are special" message. From the cradle we're inundated with the idea that we are to highly esteem ourselves. Don't get me wrong. I agree that we're special, each a unique creation of a God who loves us. But the message has so often been funneled through the pride side of our thinking. Let's talk about "me, me, ME." And that does not make for pure thinking.

It's what God thinks of us that makes us special, not what we think of ourselves. What does God think of you? He thinks you are to die for. Literally. The beautiful message of John 3:16 is that "God loved the world so much that he gave his one and only Son, so that everyone who believes in him will not perish but have eternal life" (NLT[b]).

Every single thing in us that's good is only good through Jesus, who gave us eternal life and a right standing before God by his amazing, selfless, sacrificial death. Right thinking about the Lord and about how he sees us will humble the prideful. And it will lift up the humiliated.

Full Esteem Ahead

We're instructed in Philippians not to highly esteem ourselves but to esteem others—to think of them as more important. We get ahead spiritually when "other-esteem" takes precedence over self-esteem. "Let nothing be done through selfish ambition or conceit, but in lowliness of mind let each esteem others better than himself. Let each of you look out not only for his own interests, but also for the interests of others" (Phil. 2:3–4 NKJV).

Who is our example of pure, right self-thought? Jesus! Look at the next verses in that Philippians passage:

> Think of yourselves the way Christ Jesus thought of himself. He had equal status with God but didn't think so much of himself that he had to cling to the advantages of that status no matter what. Not at all. When the time came, he set aside the privileges of deity and took on the status of a slave, became human! Having become human, he stayed human. It was an incredibly humbling process. He didn't claim special privileges. Instead, he lived a selfless, obedient life and then died a selfless, obedient death—and the worst kind of death at that—a crucifixion.
>
> Philippians 2:5–8 Message

When You Get That Sinking Feeling

When we get esteem issues backward and upside-down, we have a worse-than-quicksand kind of mess. Where do we find the balance between "God must be bragging about me to his angels today—I'll bet I'm about the best work he's ever done" and "God must be sorely disappointed in me—surely I can't be what he had in mind when he created me"?

Balance is found when we take our eyes off ourselves altogether. When we look at the holiness of God, love him, worship him, serve him, find delight in serving people in his name, then we can find the right balance. Self-loving is not the answer. Self-loathing isn't either—and it's downright depressing. I need to understand that I'm not the center of the universe. I'm not dirt either. And it's our heavenly Father who can balance our self-thought at the very point we surrender it to him.

*O Lord, transform our self-view into a balanced and
healthy one. Bring us down a notch or two where
pride has crept in. Lift us up where we're not happy
to be in our own company. Take our focus off of self
completely. Place our affection and attention solely
on you. Teach us to serve you by serving people
instead of waiting to be served by others and instead
of thinking we're unworthy to serve. Give us balance.
And let our equilibrium be you, you, YOU.*

There truly is balance in that place of surrender. And it brings
great peace. Oversized peace, even. But no need for a flag.

Therefore, I urge you, brothers, in view of God's mercy, to offer your
bodies as living sacrifices, holy and pleasing to God—this is your spiritual act of worship. Do not conform any longer to the pattern of this
world, but be transformed by the renewing of your mind. Then you
will be able to test and approve what God's will is—his good, pleasing
and perfect will. For by the grace given me I say to every one of you:
Do not think of yourself more highly than you ought, but rather think
of yourself with sober judgment, in accordance with the measure of
faith God has given you. Just as each of us has one body with many
members, and these members do not all have the same function, so
in Christ we who are many form one body, and each member belongs
to all the others. We have different gifts, according to the grace given
us. If a man's gift is prophesying, let him use it in proportion to his
faith. If it is serving, let him serve; if it is teaching, let him teach; if it
is encouraging, let him encourage; if it is contributing to the needs
of others, let him give generously; if it is leadership, let him govern
diligently; if it is showing mercy, let him do it cheerfully. Love must
be sincere. Hate what is evil; cling to what is good. Be devoted to one
another in brotherly love. Honor one another above yourselves.

Romans 12:1–10

"Keep your minds on whatever is . . . pure"

PART 3

"KEEP YOUR MINDS ON WHATEVER IS . . . RIGHT"

Is That a Necklace 11 or a Disco Ball?

Letting His Peace Rule

Have you ever had one of those necklaces that looked great at the jewelry counter, but the second you bought it, got it home, and tried it on, you realized that instead of a dignified accessory, you'd purchased something that looked like a Rottweiler collar? I realize there are teens who would much prefer the dog collar, but anything remotely canine is just not my style.

I had one necklace that was so bulky, it looked more like a cervical collar. I felt very spinally protected when I wore it, but it gave me an overstated Cleopatra kind of look. Just too much necklace. Every time I put it on, it looked like I had no neck. Necklace is one thing, but neck-less?

Even though I'm known for loving to "dress for excess," last week I decided to give that necklace up and toss the giant thing out. Being the beefy necklace that it is, I hoped it wouldn't need its own individual trash pickup day. Which is the appropriate recycle container for a necklace the size of a disco ball?

Talking Trash

I have to admit, it would bother me to give up a day of trash pickup for just one hunk of jewelry. A few weeks ago, whichever of the kids who had the job of rolling the garbage can out to the street must've gotten a little sidetracked and the can never made it out. It can get desperate around our house when we miss a week of trash pickup. Why? It's because . . . well . . . how else can I say this? . . . we are really trashy people. I'm amazed at how much garbage one family can generate.

That put us in a particular ugly trash bind that week. Not only did it leave that little layer of milk coagulating another week in the bottom of those milk jugs, but there was an overflow situation that was anything but pretty. The flies love it. But picture me weighing all my kids to see which one is the heaviest, then sending that one out to climb into the bin and stomp all the trash down to make room for more. I can just picture one of my neighbors looking out a window at just the wrong moment and saying something like, "Oh look, Bob. That lady across the street is throwing away yet another one of her children."

You know, I do hate it when I have to pick black banana peels out of my kids' hair and scrape chewed gum off their knees.

Taking Out the Spiritual Trash

For the record, I'm not as casual about spiritual trash. Letting sin sit around too long is so much worse than that milk in the bottom of the jug. We need to love right living and hate the evil garbage. That's the only way to live a clean, satisfied, joyful life.

The psalmist says it so well in Psalm 97:10–12: "People who love the Lord hate evil. The Lord watches over those who follow him and frees them from the power of the wicked. Light shines on those who do right; joy belongs to those who are honest. Rejoice in the Lord, you who do right. Praise his holy name" (NCV).

Out with the trash, in with right living! There is rejoicing every time we choose right over evil. And that trash-free "right" life? It's a life overflowing with joy.

How Does It Work?

So how do we get to that place of right living? Colossians 3:12–15 gives us some great instruction in just that:

> Therefore, as God's chosen people, holy and dearly loved, clothe your-selves with compassion, kindness, humility, gentleness and patience. Bear with each other and forgive whatever grievances you may have against one another. Forgive as the Lord forgave you. And over all these virtues put on love, which binds them all together in perfect unity. Let the peace of Christ rule in your hearts, since as members of one body you were called to peace.

It's kind of funny. The Lord seemed to keep me buried in this passage for the longest time. There was a period of about three years where the Lord wouldn't let me out of these verses. I knew it needed to be part of my quiet time if I was going to be equipped for the day. It's how I got dressed spiritually every morning. If I got up and got going without my Colossians 3, I felt spiritually naked.

The passage is full of right thinking—the rightest! It's the kind of right thinking that leads us to right living. It gives us a charge with the wonderful reminder of how dearly loved we are by the Father. What peace there is in resting in his love!

Because of his great love for us, he tells us in the passage right before this one to take off all that sinful junk. It's destructive and hurtful, and he hates that. But the Lord doesn't simply tell us to take off all those trashy things, then leave us standing there in our spiritual drawers. No, he tells us exactly what the best-dressed child of God is to wear.

Peace-wear

He tells us to put on compassion, kindness, humility, gentleness, patience, forgiveness, and love if we want to dress for spiritual success and if we want to know his peace.

Even though the Lord kept me engrossed in this passage for about three years, I still missed one word in the next verse for most of that time. When it finally popped off the page, I was rocked by its message. Verse 15 says to "let the peace of Christ rule in your heart." It was as if suddenly that little word "let" held new power for every peace pursuit. I realized that I have a big part in the peace I do or don't experience. I have to *let*.

As a believer in Christ, he put everlasting peace right there in my heart. That's really what salvation does—it gives us peace with God through Christ. But then I have a choice in every single situation I face. I can choose to fret and worry, or I can choose to *let* his peace rule. I can choose unforgiveness and bitterness, or I can *let* his peace rule. I can choose anger or agitation or impatience, or I can *let* his peace rule. I have a choice.

Wouldn't it be great if I could tell you I always make the right one? But I confess there are times I fail to "let," and I choose anger over peace. Or I let fear rule instead of peace; I choose to let worry rule instead of letting his peace rule; I let the flesh rule instead of letting his peace rule.

I don't want to settle for crummy substitutes.

> *O Lord, may I more consistently respond to you in*
> *surrender, to LET your peace rule in every situation.*
> *What joy there is waiting for me at every "let."*

To keep our minds on whatever is right and to live according to what is right in God's thinking, it's out with the sin-laced, spiritual trash, in with letting his peace rule.

Oh, and on the physical trash side, the collection guy may be a little late this week. I think the Cleopatra necklace clogged his truck.

Clothe yourselves therefore, as God's own chosen ones (His own picked representatives), [who are] purified and holy and well-beloved [by God Himself, by putting on behavior marked by] tenderhearted pity and mercy, kind feeling, a lowly opinion of yourselves, gentle ways, [and] patience [which is tireless and long-suffering, and has the power to endure whatever comes, with good temper]. Be gentle and forbearing with one another and, if one has a difference (a grievance or complaint) against another, readily pardoning each other; even as the Lord has [freely] forgiven you, so must you also [forgive]. And above all these [put on] love and enfold yourselves with the bond of perfectness [which binds everything together completely in ideal harmony]. And let the peace (soul harmony which comes) from Christ rule (act as umpire continually) in your hearts [deciding and settling with finality all questions that arise in your minds, in that peaceful state] to which as [members of Christ's] one body you were also called [to live].

Colossians 3:12–15 AMP

ALL THAT GLITTERS IS 12 NOT BULLION

Becoming a Slave to Right

I've always believed that gold and silver were for buying and wearing, not buying and selling. I don't think I'll ever become a slave to scoping the market, having to check the numbers or check my watch, listening for a closing bell. I don't want to have to figure what's up and what's down. No stock market prison for this jewelry lover, no siree.

I should probably mention, though, that there may be more of an accessory/prison connection than we might think. Think how closely "jailer" and "jeweler" are. And someone pointed out to me that one of them watches cells and the other sells watches.

To Market, to Market

I'll just confess that I know absolutely nothing about the stock market. Personally, I have a hard enough time just trying to figure out how to preheat my oven. The stock market confuses me a gazillion times more than that—though I figure if I set the market at about 350, that should be close enough for whatever's cooking.

Those market ups and downs, bulls, bears, and bouncing bonds? It all sounds about as much like a rodeo as it does share trading to me.

Responding to the Bonding

Isn't it funny, though, that Paul called himself a "bondservant" several times? It had nothing to do with trading bullion on the stock market. He had actually made himself a slave to Jesus.

That's exactly what we need to do if we're to think on things that are right. We're directed to think on the Father's idea of right, not our own. And we are the most at peace when we come under the authority of his perfect way of thinking.

Okay, so I don't know much about the stock market, but I do know that the stock market is where bonds are traded. The life of right thinking, the life of following Christ, is a little like that too. It's where "bonds" are traded. We were slaves to sin, now we're slaves to righteousness, slaves to Christ. We've traded sin bonds for the righteous bonds. Hey, now there's a smart market exchange!

Let's exchange that old way of thinking for thinking right. The first verse in the chapter where our focal passage is found says, "So stand strong in the Lord as I have told you" (Phil. 4:1 NCV). The "so" refers back to the third chapter of Philippians where we are instructed to set our sights on becoming like Christ.

The Greek word that's translated "stand strong" was often used in military contexts. Think "Rambo standing guard." If our sights are set on becoming like Christ, and that aim is guarded in the most diligent military fashion, the result will be a concrete understanding of righteousness and its place in our thinking and our behavior. Even more than thinking right and doing right, we need to be geared up and ready to become a *slave* to right—a slave to Christ.

The Right Kind of Speculation

When we're thinking right, it becomes crystal clear that slavery to Christ ushers in unsurpassed freedom. Look at what Paul said in Romans 6:15–18:

> So, since we're out from under the old tyranny, does that mean we can live any old way we want? Since we're free in the freedom of God, can we do anything that comes to mind? Hardly. You know well enough from your own experience that there are some acts of so-called freedom that destroy freedom. Offer yourselves to sin, for instance, and it's your last free act. But offer yourselves to the ways of God and the freedom never quits. All your lives you've let sin tell you what to do. But thank God you've started listening to a new master, one whose commands set you free to live openly in his freedom!
>
> Message

Freedom in our slavery? I love the way the market works in God's blessed economy.

In verses 20 and 21, Paul sums up the dead-end life of being a slave to sin:

> As long as you did what you felt like doing, ignoring God, you didn't have to bother with right thinking or right living, or right anything for that matter. But do you call that a free life? What did you get out of it? Nothing you're proud of now. Where did it get you? A dead end.
>
> Message

Who Ya Gonna Serve?

No one enjoys that dead-end life for long. Serving sin always leads to misery. And just in case you may cringe a little at the thought of surrendering yourself into slavery, keep in mind that whatever or whoever you choose to serve, you're still a slave. Not serving is not a choice. We serve sin or we serve righteousness.

Slave to sin? Slave to death? No thanks. I choose to serve the holy, holy, holy God. Paul said in the verse right before, "You used to let the different parts of your body be slaves of your evil thoughts. But now you must make every part of your body serve God, so that you will belong completely to him" (Rom. 6:19 CEV). Ahhh. Belonging. It's such a peace-inspiring thought. I belong. I belong to him! Nothing is better than recognizing that we belong to a perfect, loving Father. What blessing there is in that sweet belonging!

Proverbs 21:20–21 says, "There are precious treasures and oil in the dwelling of the wise, but a self-confident and foolish man swallows it up and wastes it. He who earnestly seeks after and craves righteousness, mercy, and loving-kindness will find life in addition to righteousness (uprightness and right standing with God) and honor" (AMP). Riches in oil? The bank? The stock market? Those are okay. But life-changing wisdom comes as we follow what is right—believe it, think it, do it. And thinking right and living right are like cornering the market on the peaceful, good life!

Let's make it a goal to constantly take stock of our thinking and of how and who we surrender our thoughts and our lives to. And by the way, this kind of "taking stock" will not necessarily call for capital investors.

I'm using this freedom language because it's easy to picture. You can readily recall, can't you, how at one time the more you did just what you felt like doing—not caring about others, not caring about God—the worse your life became and the less freedom you had? And how much different is it now as you live in God's freedom, your lives healed and expansive in holiness? . . .

But now that you've found you don't have to listen to sin tell you what to do, and have discovered the delight of listening to God telling you, what a surprise! A whole, healed, put-together life right now, with more and more of life on the way! Work hard for sin your whole life and your pension is death. But God's gift is real life, eternal life, delivered by Jesus, our Master.

Romans 6:19, 22–23 Message

A LITTLE JADED 13

What Living Right Does for Those Who See

It's hard to get new bling without running to a girlfriend who loves you and saying, "Looky what I got!" You can always tell a true friend when you have a new piece of jewelry. She's the one who will ooh and aah over your jade with diamond trim without gritting her teeth.

Asking someone to look is one thing. But please tell me you're not one of those people who shoves the milk gallon under the nose of a friend or family member and says, "Hey, would you smell this?" The sense of smell is one of the only senses that can be used a little like a weapon. Asking someone to smell your new cologne or your fresh-baked apple pie? Nice. But ask someone to sniff the milk and suddenly you could be instigating war. Chemical warfare, no less.

Need to know which items fall in the "never ask anyone to smell this" category? Here are my publishable top ten.

Top 10 Sniff Questions You Should Never Ask

1. Could you sniff this and tell me if you think I can get another month's wear out of it?

2. I can't tell if this is a fresh coconut or an old cantaloupe—could you take a sniff?
3. Could you please sniff this pit and tell me if my new deodorant is working?
4. Okay, now how about this pit?
5. Could you sniff my laundry room and tell me if you think other people can tell I have this many cats?
6. Would you sniff this now that I've put out the flames and tell me if it smells burned to you?
7. Would you take a whiff of this and tell me if you think there's anything Dr. Scholl's can do for me?
8. Would you let me squirt a little of this stuff on you, then sniff it and tell me if you think it would chase you off if you were attacking me and I sprayed it in your face?
9. Does this smell radioactive to you?
10. Would you sniff this and tell me if you think it's still milk or if I should now classify it as *cheese*?

Sniff unto Others as You Would Have Them Sniff unto You

Why is it that there are those who see chunks in the milk, and *being unwilling to sniff the stuff themselves,* they try to pawn the stench off on someone else?

"I don't want to smell this—it might be disgusting. Here, you do it."

Or they come across questionable socks lying in limbo between the clean pile and the dirty pile of laundry, and fearing their own nose hairs might be singed off, they ask you to sniff instead.

Note to all my friends and family: I'll look at your jade, your opals—your rubies, sapphires, and diamonds too. But please don't ask me to sniff your socks.

As a matter of fact, there should be a standing universal rule of etiquette that says you should never ask anyone to smell something you're not willing to smell yourself.

Something Doesn't Smell Right

On the spiritual side, anytime we encourage people to think right and live right when we're not living it ourselves, we're definitely sniffing up the wrong tree there too. We need to make it our own personal universal rule to follow the Creator of the universe out of love for him—it's the right thing to do.

To think on the things that are right in the context of Philippians 4:8 is to line up our thinking with our heavenly Father's divine standard of rightness and holiness. How "right" does God think? He is always right, always just, perfectly holy.

Not only is it the right thing to do, it's a testimony that prompts those around us to right living to boot. Psalm 106:2 asks the question, "Who can proclaim the mighty acts of the LORD or fully declare his praise?" Then the psalmist answers the question in the next verse: "Blessed are they who maintain justice, who constantly do what is right." When we do what is right, we're proclaiming the mighty acts of the Lord and we're declaring his praise. Showing off new bling may be fun for a moment, but it's absolutely nothing compared to the enduring pleasure of showing off our amazing God and proclaiming his name.

This Could Raise a Stink

Don't expect others to live right if you're not. Your children included. We'll look at following examples and becoming good examples ourselves more in later chapters, and I know not all my readers are moms, but could you indulge me in a little mommy-minute here for those who are?

We need to continually be thinking about what kind of example we're setting. Is it an example of thinking right and living right? We generally love our children so very much that it feels like our hearts are going to jump right out of our bodies. Do we love them enough to live rightness before them?

Proverbs 22:6 says to "train up a child in the way he should go, and when he is old he will not depart from it" (NKJV). We're instructed to train them, to invest time and energy in pouring good, solid teaching into their lives. And it's our responsibility as parents to train them in godliness—in right thinking and right living. But a mom can't share what she doesn't have. Is your relationship with God your Father vital, real, and exciting? Does it smell good, as it were? Is it a life that is so appealing that your children are thrilled at the prospect of having a life just like yours? It's impossible to teach your kids to have a vital relationship with the Lord if you don't.

A Sweet-Smelling Offering

Share with your children often what God is doing in your life and the blessings you find in thinking right and living right. Tell them stories of how God has blessed. That blesses them, and it's a sweet-smelling praise offering to the Lord. And tell them other stories too, ones where you admit the times you've failed. Ask them to forgive you when it's called for. It's astounding what they can learn from that one act of humility alone, but when you add it to your other God-sharing and your right living, you're encouraging them in the right life too.

Make a personal rule of consistently doing what is right.

Of course, back on the olfactory side, I'm thinking it's also a good idea to make it a personal rule that if you see chunks in the milk, you shouldn't even bother sniffing. Just have some coffee.

> These are the commands, decrees and laws the LORD your God directed me to teach you to observe in the land that you are crossing the Jordan to possess, so that you, your children and their children after them may fear the LORD your God as long as you live by keeping all his decrees and commands that I give you, and so that you may enjoy long life. Hear, O Israel, and be careful to obey so that it may go well with you and that you may increase greatly in a land flowing with milk and honey, just as the LORD, the God of your fathers, promised

you. Hear, O Israel: The LORD our God, the LORD is one. Love the LORD your God with all your heart and with all your soul and with all your strength. These commandments that I give you today are to be upon your hearts. Impress them on your children. Talk about them when you sit at home and when you walk along the road, when you lie down and when you get up. Tie them as symbols on your hands and bind them on your foreheads. Write them on the doorframes of your houses and on your gates.

Deuteronomy 6:1–9

TAKING OUR 14 ACCESSORIES AT FACE VALUE

The Value of Beauty, Self, Others

Is it true accessories are only as pleasant as the face they're surrounding? If so, does that mean we have to take all our accessories at face value?

It's a bit frustrating that my face has been choosing its own accessories the past couple of years. It doesn't even ask my opinion. A decorative line across the forehead. An ornamental fold at the jowl. And sadly, you could drive a truck into these pores. The older I get, the more ornamentation I'm dealing with. These are accessories I never counted on. So does this mean my face value is depreciating?

On an episode of one of those extreme face makeover kind of shows, I saw an entire team of specialists working to increase the "face value" of a middle-aged woman. Out with the lines, away with the jowls; sanding pores and slicing and dicing from hairline to neck. Pretty amazing.

I know what you're thinking, but I'm afraid those surgeries are probably not a viable option for me. Why? Because I have an allergy. I'm extremely allergic to pain. Exposure to pain causes profuse, acute whining.

Do I Need a Dermatologist or Nuclear Physicist?

After one of the procedures on the woman, I was surprised to see that she was positively glowing. No, I don't mean happy-glowing. Not even beauty-glowing. I mean that her face was sort of a radiant pink/red. They said they had given her a chemical peel. Good to know—since I was thinking instead she might've been messing around with radioactive isotopes of some kind. And then fallen into them face-first.

I don't know, maybe that's close to what happened. All I can say is that it must've been some peel. Her teeth were showing . . . with her mouth closed. Having shimmering accessories is one thing, but a radioactive face shimmer just doesn't seem right. I'd rather shine without the plutonium, thanks.

A Few Layers In

No need for radioactive isotopes or any other chemicals when it's time to peel away a few layers in our thinking. There's peace waiting for me when I realize that I am not my face. When God looks at me, he doesn't see wrinkles, flaps, or giant pores. He doesn't look on the outward appearance at all. And you are not your looks. "For the LORD does not see as man sees; for man looks at the outward appearance, but the LORD looks at the heart" (1 Sam. 16:7 NKJV).

If you've given your life to Christ, when God looks at you, that's who he sees. Jesus. Knowing who I am and how God sees me results in the right kind of thinking, the right kind of fallout. No uranium needed.

Radiating Grace

There's also peace in right thinking about who others are and in learning to think of them as God does. Who wants to be two-faced? Wouldn't that require twice the chemicals anyway? No thanks! Instead, there's peace when I embrace right thinking about how God sees me as well as how he sees others. There is peace when I choose to show his grace to others.

A life of hypocrisy yields the exact opposite of peace. The turmoil of a critical spirit, the unrest of envy, the upheaval of jealousy, the stress and dissatisfaction of living a fakey, fakey life. Want a life of peace? Sometimes it first requires surgery. It's a spiritual surgery: a plank-ectomy. Jesus spelled it out for us in Matthew 7:1–5 when he said,

> Do not judge, or you too will be judged. For in the same way you judge others, you will be judged, and with the measure you use, it will be measured to you. Why do you look at the speck of sawdust in your brother's eye and pay no attention to the plank in your own eye? How can you say to your brother, "Let me take the speck out of your eye," when all the time there is a plank in your own eye? You hypocrite, first take the plank out of your own eye, and then you will see clearly to remove the speck from your brother's eye.

Instead of judging others, we need to value others the way Jesus does, not look down our noses because they stumble the same way we do.

Let's Face It

What gave the lady on the extreme makeover show her value? A new face? That's not how God sees it. What gives me value? Getting rid of pores that look like manhole covers? What a temporary kind of gauge. What truly gives us value? It's our life in Christ.

Faces come and go. Literally, in some instances. Only our souls are eternal. And it's what we do with Jesus that makes the soul difference. Focusing on and treasuring looks—or anything temporal for that matter—will leave us defeated and deflated. We need to treasure the right things.

Incommunicado on the Avocado

What we treasure is so often in the eye of the beholder. To me, for instance, a side of guacamole is a thing of beauty. As far as my husband is concerned, if it's green and it's slimy enough to slide down the side of the burrito, it might as well be a side of pond algae.

I try to hide avocado dip from him so he won't feel compelled to bury it somewhere. One person's treasure is another person's compost.

Jesus said, "For where your treasure is, there your heart will be also," (Matt. 6:21). What we treasure gets our passion, our attention, our "heart." That's why we have to be ultra careful what we treasure. And it's Jesus who should always be our one true treasure.

Treasuring Beauty?

Treasuring beauty is placing our heart in an unstable place. Proverbs 31:30–31 says,

> Charm and grace are deceptive, and beauty is vain [because it is not lasting], but a woman who reverently and worshipfully fears the Lord, she shall be praised! Give her of the fruit of her hands, and let her own works praise her in the gates [of the city]!
>
> AMP

Beauty is fleeting, no matter how much we may slice and dice. If we base our value on looks, our peace is in grave danger. Where is that life of praise? We find it in reverently and worshipfully fearing, honoring, loving the Lord.

Thinking in the right direction about my own value and the value of others is essential for a life of peace. More emphasis on him, maybe a little less on wrinkle reduction? Sounds like the best beauty plan to me. And even if I ever do go for a chemical peel, I'd prefer everyone in the room keep all their isotopes to themselves, thank you. I think we may have something with the guacamole, though. Instead of "letting it slide," we could make it into a mask. I hear it reduces the appearance of manhole-sized pores.

> The integrity of the upright will guide them, but the perversity of the unfaithful will destroy them. Riches do not profit in the day of wrath, but righteousness delivers from death. The righteousness of the blameless will direct his way aright, but the wicked will fall by his own wickedness. The righteousness of the upright will deliver them, but the unfaithful will be caught by their lust.
>
> Proverbs 11:3–6 NKJV

Shining Time 15

Effervescing Hope, Wisdom

I went to an author event recently that was a "bring out the big bling" event. You know how I love to shine, so I put on a necklace that looked something like a brass dinner plate and further embellished with earrings that could've doubled as matching wind chimes. *Blingety-bling-bling-bling.*

Talk about shining. Between my multiple tonnage of the brass bling and the extra-bright party lights, I must admit I felt like I could've been a conduit for a laser beam. I wondered if I might need to wear a warning label:

CAUTION: Do not look directly into the accessories. Corneal damage may occur.

Guard your retinas, people. Laser bling coming through.

Magnetic Personality

At least I wasn't the only one. There was so much metal that one strong multi-metal magnet could've shifted two-thirds of the party to one corner of the room. I noticed a few women who looked like they could've been heading to a Star Trek convention. I couldn't tell if they were wearing bling, com badges, or some kind of cybernetic enhancements and other robot/android limbs. I may have even seen a communicator or two. And maybe it was the power of suggestion, but I could've sworn I heard someone speaking Klingon. That's when I started to wonder if I could just have Scotty lock onto my signal and beam me directly to the buffet. Anyway, I always loved the swirling-glitter look of beaming in and out. With as much bling as I was toting, I could shine coming and going.

Keep Shining

In a sort of similarly shiny situation, a stranger gave me a shining compliment the other day. She said she thought I had a bubbly personality. Wasn't that sweet?

I appreciated the thought, really I did. But then I couldn't stop trying to define the bubbles. I found myself thinking about Alka-Seltzer. I know, how weird am I? But I wondered if a bubbly personality is really the ideal. I know that the Alka-Seltzer stuff works for a lot of people, but no matter how hard I've tried, I have never been able to completely swallow stomach medicine that looks like it's boiling. When my stomach is churning, why would I take a medicine that's already churning on its own? Isn't that double churning? And wouldn't double churning make *butter*? Believe me, not everything is better with Blue Bonnet on it.

Bubble-Butter

If I'm going to bubble, I want to bubble with all the right kinds of bubbles. In Romans 15:13, Paul talks about God filling us to the point of bubbling over: "May the God of hope fill you with all joy and peace as you trust in him, so that you may overflow with hope by the power of the Holy Spirit." He fills us with joy and peace, and then we overflow with hope. Effervescing hope. Now that's the way to bubble.

Sadly, too many times we women—even those of us who've surrendered our lives to Christ—overflow with anything but hope. Why would we choose to brim over with despair?

We're told to keep our minds on what is right—and what is true and pure and holy, what is friendly and proper, worthwhile and praiseworthy. If we're to succeed in thinking on these right things and if we're to experience the resulting peace, we must continually think along these positive lines. And that means we need to make a conscious effort to stop thinking along negative lines, to stop letting our thoughts get stuck in a negative downdraft that traps us in thoughts that are exactly the opposite of right and pure, friendly and worthwhile.

Sulking in the Night or Dancing in the Light?

We live in a fallen world. It's a dark place. Things are anything but perfect here. I would venture to say you have at least 100 reasons to sit in a dark corner and sulk at this very moment. I would further venture to say that you have at least 100,000 reasons to flick on the light and dance. So often in life, you get to choose.

Negative, gloomy-Gus thinking breeds more negative, gloomy-Gus thinking. Don't start a pattern of miserable thoughts. It's unwise to head in that desolate direction, especially when you know that it could drag you down like quicksand. Have you ever tried to dance in quicksand? There's no dancing, no bubbling, no shining.

In a sense, this thought entirely sums up our focal passage for this book. Think on things that are true, pure, right, holy, friendly, proper, worthwhile, and worthy of praise. Or get stuck in everything negative. You get to choose. And where you choose to keep your thoughts on a regular basis—positive or negative—has a direct result on the peace you will or will not experience.

It has a direct result on the peace you bring into the lives of others as well. Continuous negative thoughts will make you a negative, hopeless person, and you'll likely find yourself experiencing a desperate friend shortage. Who wants to be around a person who is such a hopeless downer? Positive thoughts will make you a more positive person, the kind of person who shines joy to those around—and that will draw people to you quicker than a multi-metal magnet. People love to be near effervescing hope. They love to have some of that hope spill over onto them and into their own lives. And when we're thinking in the most positive directions, we love to be ones who God is using to overflow his hope onto everyone around. There's the best kind of dancing there.

Overflowing the hope of God and thinking right and positive thoughts is the wise way to live. The wisdom and insight of God is something we need to passionately seek if we want to live a peaceful life.

Panning for Peace

God's Word encourages us to search for wisdom as if we were searching for treasure.

> That's right—if you make Insight your priority, and won't take no for an answer, Searching for it like a prospector panning for gold, like an adventurer on a treasure hunt, Believe me, before you know it

Fear-of-God will be yours; you'll have come upon the Knowledge of God. And here's why: God gives out Wisdom free, is plainspoken in Knowledge and Understanding. He's a rich mine of Common Sense for those who live well, a personal bodyguard to the candid and sincere. He keeps his eye on all who live honestly, and pays special attention to his loyally committed ones.

Proverbs 2:3–8 Message

Wisely thinking the best things and continually seeking the wisdom of God really can build our peace and our hope too. I think I'll shoot for having a bubbly peace and hope.

Anyway, that gal who told me I had a bubbly personality? I wonder if she was just trying to butter me up.

Celebrate God all day, every day. I mean, revel in him! Make it as clear as you can to all you meet that you're on their side, working with them and not against them. Help them see that the Master is about to arrive. He could show up any minute! Don't fret or worry. Instead of worrying, pray. Let petitions and praises shape your worries into prayers, letting God know your concerns. Before you know it, a sense of God's wholeness, everything coming together for good, will come and settle you down. It's wonderful what happens when Christ displaces worry at the center of your life. Summing it all up, friends, I'd say you'll do best by filling your minds and meditating on things true, noble, reputable, authentic, compelling, gracious—the best, not the worst; the beautiful, not the ugly; things to praise, not things to curse. Put into practice what you learned from me, what you heard and saw and realized. Do that, and God, who makes everything work together, will work you into his most excellent harmonies.

Philippians 4:4–9 Message

PART 4

"KEEP YOUR MINDS ON WHATEVER IS . . . HOLY"

INK-BLING 16

Surrendering in Obedience to Holy Living

It's a beautiful idea: ink-bling. I was given the nicest gift. It was a pen covered in a gazillion colorful, shiny stones. Cute and practical! Even better, it was on a chain so I could wear it around my neck. I always thought soap on a rope was a nifty idea, but a pen on a rope is so much better. And this was not your basic useful item hanging around my neck. It was bling! Wearing a pen as jewelry makes it more than just a writing tool. More than just an accessory. Suddenly I found myself accessor-writing. And I liked it.

That pen was practical in more ways than one. My favorite pen always has a way of disappearing. Unless, of course, I'm wearing it. I lose pens long before they run out of ink. But not this one. It was good to the last drop. How sad when I finally had to let it go. Especially since I didn't have the slightest inkling where to get another one. (*Ink*-ling? You have to love a bad pen-pun, don't you?)

Write This Down

What do you do when you have a pen that won't write? If you're like most of us, you sling it a few times in that stabbing motion, hoping gravity is going to somehow jar the ink loose (I wonder if that's ever really worked for anyone). Then you scribble. Then you scribble bigger and faster. Then frustration builds and you scribble harder. Then harder. You scribble until you tear a hole in the paper. Then you throw the pen. Then you look around to see if anyone saw you throw the pen. Then while you're feeling silly about throwing the pen, you pick it up and pretend it just slipped out of your hand (yeah, sure—it slipped out of your hand and spontaneously flew across the room). Then you shrug and smile and put the pen in your purse.

Later you get home to find that the pen leaked and left a giant splotch of blue on the front of your favorite handbag. Why can't a pen simply do its job without making a mess?

Inking and Thinking in Holy Directions

I wonder if God ever asks that question about me. I think I'm a bit of a pen hypocrite. I'll judge the pen for not consistently delivering and for making messes, but if I get honest, I'll admit there are entirely too many times when I'm not consistent in the things the Lord has shown me. And even though I'm not where I know I should be or I'm not doing the things he's already shown me to do, I'm fussing and scribbling because life isn't unfolding the way I planned. What a mess—a mess that I've made with my own hand. And the "ink" ends up everywhere except where it was intended.

We're instructed to keep our minds on whatever is holy. The word used here for "holiness" in the original language describes being morally clean, pure, and undefiled.

Life is much less messy when we stay away from impurity and stay consistent in his Word and consistent in those things he's called us to do. I know: doi! No big revelation there. But sometimes it's the simplest things that give us the most trouble. And it's neglecting those simple disciplines that can leave us frustrated at the end of the day—big ink stain and no eternal fruit.

Back to the Holy Handbook

How do we know how to live in holiness, think in holiness, and stay away from sin? Second Timothy 3:16–17 says,

> All Scripture is inspired by God and is useful to teach us what is true and to make us realize what is wrong in our lives. It corrects us when we are wrong and teaches us to do what is right. God uses it to prepare and equip his people to do every good work.
>
> NLT[b]

Disobedience keeps us from living the Spirit-filled life. When we're surrendered to Christ and walking in obedience, his Spirit fills us and accomplishes great things. We're the pen. He is the ink.

Andrew Murray, in *The Deeper Christian Life*, reminds us that we are called to surrender in obedience:

> Blessed is the man who knows what it is to be nothing, to be just an empty vessel meet for God's use. You cannot expect to be filled with the Spirit unless you want to live for Christ's Kingdom. You cannot expect all the love and peace and joy of heaven to come into your life and be your treasures, unless you give them up absolutely to the Kingdom of God, and possess and use them only for Him. It is the soul utterly given up to God that will receive in its emptying the fullness of the Holy Spirit.[1]

Out of God's Will and into the Fish

Jonah was one who lost his peace by choosing to disobey God. Jonah 1:1–3 says,

> Now the word of the LORD came to Jonah the son of Amittai, saying, "Arise, go to Nineveh, that great city, and cry out against it; for their wickedness has come up before Me." But Jonah arose to flee to Tarshish from the presence of the LORD. He went down to Joppa, and found a ship going to Tarshish; so he paid the fare, and

went down into it, to go with them to Tarshish from the presence of the Lord.

NKJV

Flee from the presence of the Lord? Really, Jonah? Where exactly *isn't* the Lord? Psalm 139:7–10 says,

> Where can I go from your Spirit?
>> Where can I flee from your presence?
> If I go up to the heavens, you are there;
>> if I make my bed in the depths, you are there.
> If I rise on the wings of the dawn,
>> if I settle on the far side of the sea,
> even there your hand will guide me,
>> your right hand will hold me fast.

We can't hide from God. But it is true that the moment we choose to disobey, our fellowship with him is broken. His presence? Can't sense it. The peace he gives? Totally gone. Fruitfulness? None. We might as well be a pen with no ink. Empty and useless.

Saved in Sweet Surrender

What does it take to get from disobedience and the peace-less belly of a fish to contentedly walking again in the presence of the Lord? From inside the fish, Jonah prayed,

> When my life was ebbing away,
>> I remembered you, Lord,
>> and my prayer rose to you,
>> to your holy temple.
> Those who cling to worthless idols
>> forfeit the grace that could be theirs.
> But I, with a song of thanksgiving,
>> will sacrifice to you.

What I have vowed I will make good.
Salvation comes from the LORD.

Jonah 2:7–9

Jonah knew where to find salvation. It was in his surrender. He had been filled with his own desires—what he wanted, instead of what God wanted. And as soon as Jonah made that surrender, *patooey!* The next verse says, "And the LORD commanded the fish, and it vomited Jonah onto dry land" (v. 10).

Life Lessons to Stay on Dry Land

So there are lessons for us to reinforce all through this book's focal passage in Philippians. Lesson number one in this chapter: Obey God, stay morally clean. Number two is related: Stay consistent in doing the things he tells us to do in his Word and allow him to give life meaning and make it fruitful.

If you're in the belly of a fish, so to speak, are you ready to give up your life as fish food, to surrender to pure living, to surrender to his will for you, and to enjoy his presence and life-giving peace again? Make that surrender. I guarantee, it's a surrender you'll never, ever regret.

Oh, and I shouldn't forget lesson number three: A cheap pen is . . . what? . . . less than fifty cents? When it won't write, face it, you need to toss the thing and get a new one.

When the Spirit is given to us from heaven, deserts will become orchards thick as fertile forests. Honesty and justice will prosper there, and justice will produce lasting peace and security. You, the LORD's people, will live in peace, calm and secure.

Isaiah 32:15–18 CEV

17 Turn On the Bling

God Is Holy

How frustrating is it to put on your finest bling for a night at a fine restaurant, only to find the lighting is so low no one can see it? I know the subdued lighting is supposed to create a glamorous, romantic ambiance in the most high class way, but really, how glamorous are night-vision goggles? And how fine is your restaurant dining if you can't read the menu or see what you're eating after you give up and order the special? *Wait a minute, is this meatball supposed to be this crunchy or did I just swallow yet another earring?*

Mood lighting? Not so much. As a matter of fact, making my way through the dark puts me in the mood to do something closer to mining coal. If it wouldn't undermine the fashion goal, one of those coal miner's lamp-hats might be just the right accessory (tell me I'm not the only one who snickered at the use of the word "undermine" in a coal context).

Big decision. Wear the miner hat or exchange my accessories for decorating myself in Christmas lights. Maybe as a last resort I could rub two breadsticks together.

Truly Enlightened

Have you ever noticed that there's no "dark switch"? You can walk into a dark restaurant and hunt for a light switch to turn on. But how many times have you walked into a room full of light and searched for a dark switch to flick? Even a dimmer switch doesn't add darkness. It takes away light. Light switch? Yes. Dark switch? Weird idea.

If you look up *darkness* in a dictionary, you'll find that it's the "absence or deficiency of light." So can you guess what a dictionary includes in the definition for *light*? If you guessed "the absence of darkness," while that makes sense, it's not the right answer. Among definitions for light, you'll find "luminous, radiant energy." Light has substance. Darkness is the absence of that substance.

How appropriate that the Bible tells us that God is light and in him is no darkness at all. God is not the absence of something. He is *the* something. In fact, he is everything. And in everything that he is, there is holiness.

We are called to live in his light and to walk in his light, to believe that he is holy and without any darkness at all. We are called to shine his holy light through our lives in all we do. And we are called to keep our minds well lit. His light is perfect ambiance.

Scared of the Dark?

Incidentally, there's no need to fear the darkness. Avoid it, sure, but don't fear it. The God of light is so much more powerful than the prince of darkness. Ours is the God of luminous, energetic, radiating power—he is light and he's the creator of light! Colossians 1:13 tells us that God delivers us from the power of darkness.

We don't have to dwell on the darkness at all. That's one of the most life-changing aspects of the Philippians passage we're focusing on. You can choose to look to the light, to relish the light, to bask in the light of God. Every day offers a new choice to do just that. Every day is full of changes and opportunities. You've never in the past been exactly who you are today. You have the power to take a step into the light this very day.

When we stay plugged in to the source of all light, juicing up every day by spending time with him, we soak up the power to reflect his light all the more. We become illuminated by the glow. And then it spreads! In Philippians 2:15 Paul encourages us to "become blameless and harmless, children of God without fault in the midst of a crooked and perverse generation, among whom you shine as lights in the world" (NKJV).

Father of Light

Isn't it amazing that even though God is holy and set apart, even though he is light, we can have a close, loving, personal relationship with him? We can snuggle up to the light! In James 1:17 he's called "the Father of lights." Jesus himself confirmed the new kind of relationship when he was teaching his disciples to pray and he instructed them to call God "Father." What a wild and marvelous new notion that must have been for them. For all of history they had understood that God is holy and that there had always been a connection between God and his people, yet the idea of a close, personal, "dad" kind of relationship with their holy God must've all but blown them away.

We're allowed to walk into the light and become God's children not because of our talents and abilities. It's not even because of our goodness. It's all because of his great love and mercy that we can call him Father.

He is the Father who takes care of his children in the most personal way. He is the Father who offers comfort and a quiet knowing that he is always near, and that his light is the warmest, most glorious place to be. Coal miner's daughter? Nope. I'm a daughter of the Father of Light.

Fake Light

Incidentally, one of the Enemy's ploys to get us off track is to counterfeit Christ. The Bible tells us that he tries to mask his darkness, appearing as an angel of light (2 Cor. 11:14). The only thing sadder than being in the dark is being in the dark and not knowing it. Or heading straight for darkness, convinced it's light. It's like watching a bug headed straight into the zapper.

Ephesians 5:11–13 says, "And have no fellowship with the unfruitful works of darkness, but rather expose them. . . . But all things that are exposed are made manifest by the light, for whatever makes manifest is light" (NKJV).

Never be fooled into thinking you need to snuggle up to the darkness. The sinful, worldly way of thinking is deceitful—and it leads to fruitlessness and death. The holy walk God calls us to is different from the world's way of thinking. As different as night and day.

In the Light of What God Has Done

Let's keep our minds on the God who is light and who is our wonderful, loving Father. Choose to dwell on his holiness and to worship him. Understanding more about who he is through his Word is guaranteed to light up your life everywhere you go. From the fine restaurant to the fast-food drive-through, we can shine his light.

Fine dining? Not so necessary. Let's head for fine living!

> This is the verdict: Light has come into the world, but men loved darkness instead of light because their deeds were evil. Everyone who does evil hates the light, and will not come into the light for fear that his deeds will be exposed. But whoever lives by the truth comes into the light, so that it may be seen plainly that what he has done has been done through God.
>
> John 3:19–21

Looking at Life 18 through Peace-colored Glasses

Holy Living/Seeking Peace

My grandmother had reading glasses that doubled as major bling. You've never seen so many rhinestones in such a small surface area. They seemed to defy mathematical principles left and right. Not only were her glasses covered with a thoroughly impressive number of rhinestones (honestly, it was like a tiara for her face), but she wore the glasses on a shiny strap around her neck. Eyeglasses or necklace? Both! Sort of like multitasking blingage. I was so impressed.

I can just imagine my grandma's optometrist holding up eyeglasses on a sparkly cord in one hand; in the other, cordless eyeglasses that were doomed to get lost. I picture him saying, "Which is better? This? Or this?" "A? Or B?" "One? Or two?" Who wouldn't pick the eye-bling on a string?

Keep an Eye Out

Anytime she didn't wear her glasses around her neck, Grandma was constantly on a search. I couldn't help but laugh when I'd catch her on a glasses-seeking mission . . . when I could clearly see they were perched on top of her head. I did my laughing very quietly, of course—being the semi-evil child that I was, I never told her they were up there. It was just too fun to watch her rifling through her purse and emptying out drawers with the rhinestone wonders glimmering just a few inches over her eyebrows.

Seek and You Shall Find

Searching for the glasses on your head? That's still funny. But searching for peace in all the wrong places? That's oh so sad. It's sad too when we miss the fact altogether that we truly are instructed to seek after that peace.

We're told in Psalm 34:14 to "seek peace and pursue it" (NKJV). The first part of that very verse gives us an essential part of the how-to: "Depart from evil and do good." We actively seek peace when we're doing good, living well, spurning evil—living in personal holiness.

First Peter 3:10–11 says,

"KEEP YOUR MINDS ON WHATEVER IS . . . HOLY"

For let him who wants to enjoy life and see good days [good—whether apparent or not] keep his tongue free from evil and his lips from guile (treachery, deceit). Let him turn away from wickedness and shun it, and let him do right. Let him search for peace (harmony; undisturbedness from fears, agitating passions, and moral conflicts) and seek it eagerly. [Do not merely desire peaceful relations with God, with your fellowmen, and with yourself, but pursue, go after them!]

AMP

Peace-Seeking Missile

We are to pursue peace, to go after it with rocketlike zeal. Still, so many women are convinced that the way to find peace is to seek happiness. The truth is that seeking happiness will so often leave us irritated and discouraged. We simply can't find peace through seeking happiness. We find peace by seeking holiness.

Keeping our minds on whatever is "holy" will keep our focus clear—no matter what kind of glasses we're wearing—or where we're wearing them. It's quite practical to seek peace by living a holy life. And the psalmist says to the Lord he trusts in Psalm 16:11, "You will teach me how to live a holy life" (NCV). Anyone who truly seeks to live a life of peace through living a life of holiness will find that the Lord himself is faithful to be the great teacher.

Holiness? That's Deep!

Holiness can be an intimidating topic, to be sure. When I wrote the book *The Purse-uit of Holiness: Learning to Imitate the Master Designer*, every morning when I opened up the computer file to work on it, I was overwhelmed with my complete and utter unworthiness to address the subject. The focal passage in that book is 1 Peter 1:13–16:

Therefore, prepare your minds for action; be self-controlled; set your hope fully on the grace to be given you when Jesus Christ is revealed. As obedient children, do not conform to the evil desires you had when you lived in ignorance. But just as he who called you is holy, so be holy in all you do; for it is written: "Be holy, because I am holy."

Write about holiness? Me? I kept wondering if I shouldn't just stick with the chick-laughs and let the deep theologians tackle the profound matter of holiness. Purse-talk? Sure. Holiness? Gulp.

But I never felt the Lord letting me off of the holiness hook. The importance of women seeking to live in holiness wouldn't let me merely skim over it either. It still won't. Seeking peace through living a life of holiness makes all the difference. It's the difference between finding and experiencing that indescribable peace and the frustration of always hunting for it, never finding it—a scenario so much worse than never, ever finding those glasses that are sitting right there on top of your head. Boiling it down, no holiness, no peace.

He Who Is Holy Calls Us to Be Holy

According to the passage in 1 Peter, we are called to be holy because he is holy. *Holy* means "set apart." God's holiness is set apart in a different way than ours is. Ours is a pursuit of living righteously. His is a state of being—his is set apart from any other definition of holiness. His is "set-apart set-apart-ness." It's the complete, holiest of holiness.

While we'll never have God's kind of holiness, we're to be set apart too. When we've given our lives to the holy Lord, our lives should look different. We should be growing to look more and more like the one to whom we belong. It's our calling to live holy lives because he is holy. We're given the holy living charge in a nutshell in 1 Peter 1:13–16. We need to prepare our minds for action, to be self-controlled, and to do good, not evil.

As we prepare for action, exercise self-control, seek to do good, and stay away from evil, we see his holiness affecting our lives in holiness. Hey, multitasking! And when we're focused on his holiness, we find ourselves looking at life through peace-colored glasses. Rosy indeed.

Grandma's Hair-Raising Revenge

In case you're curious about how my grandma reacted to the fact that I so inconsiderately neglected to tell her that her glasses were on her head, let me tell you that the woman knew how to get her justice. It was odd that so soon after a glasses-hunting incident, it would suddenly be time for my bangs to get a "little trimming." Next thing I knew, *scalp-bangs*.

The moral: Don't mess with Grandma. Or her tiara-glasses. Laughs may come and go, but bad bangs last for weeks.

> Whoever wants to embrace life and see the day fill up with good, here's what you do: Say nothing evil or hurtful; Snub evil and cultivate good; run after peace for all you're worth. God looks on all this with approval, listening and responding well to what he's asked; But he turns his back on those who do evil things.
>
> 1 Peter 3:10–12 Message

THE ACCESSORY POOL 19

Running from Sin, Standing for Christ,
Denying the Flesh

Has anyone else noticed that accessories tend to melt outdoors? Or maybe that's my makeup. Or maybe it's my face. Whichever, it's one more reason I'm an indoor kind of gal. I know it might offend the outdoor lovers, but I like to stay safely tucked into the comfort of a climate-controlled environment where my face and/or accessories don't end up in a pool on my chest. Totally not the accessory pool I'd like to choose from, thank you very much.

Last summer, however, I spent several days outside. Not my usual place, I know, but despite the fact that they grow outside, I do love my flowers. A rumble had started between the flowers and a gang of big, ugly weeds. I had to go out and try to break it up. That last day I went outside and was delighted to see a hummingbird in my yard. Not a yard ornament. A real one. I was thinking, *What in the world is a hummingbird doing in my yard?*

Then it hit me. It wasn't actually a hummingbird. It was a mosquito. A hummingbird-sized mosquito. That sucker was big enough to ride.

Bucking Mosquito

I didn't have a saddle, so I took what I considered the most logical course of action. I ran. I really ran. I ran like a cheap pair of pantyhose. It was probably the most exercise I'd gotten all summer.

I thought about going back out with some bug spray, but I could picture the mosquito stallion laughing at my chemicals, sucking out most of my blood, then riding off into the sunset to who knows where. Not the kind of rumble I was willing to participate in. Sometimes it's probably best to donate the flowers to a wild, unbroken insect and just plain skedaddle.

It's important to know when to run. The Bible tells us to run away from temptation, for instance. Second Timothy 2:22 says, "Flee also youthful lusts; but pursue righteousness, faith, love, peace with those who call on the Lord out of a pure heart" (NKJV). Notice the peace pursuit tucked in that passage? If we want peace, we need to know when it's time to kick up some dust.

Flesh Flight

Fleeing sin is denying the flesh. You might be surprised to find out how many women are experiencing a serious lack of peace—all because they choose to indulge the flesh instead of shutting it down. In *The Deeper Christian Life*, Andrew Murray says,

> I want to come to all who are perhaps hungering and long for the better life, and asking what is wrong that you are without it, to point out that what is wrong is just one thing—*allowing the flesh to rule in you, and trusting in the power of the flesh to make you good.*[1]

Allowing your sinful nature to rule your life—or even trusting in your own self to get "good"—will never result in peace or victory. We need to wrangle in every rogue, sinful thought. Second Corinthians 10:5 says, "We capture every thought and make it give up and obey Christ" (NCV). Bust that bronco! Force that offbeat thought to holler "Uncle"!

In our focal passage, we're instructed to "keep" our minds. We're not keeping our minds if we're allowing stray sinful thoughts to capture our minds and carry our thoughts off into the sunset to who knows where. Our every thought should be accounted for. And our every thought should belong to Christ.

Fight or Flight

Sometimes we stand and fight sin. Ephesians 6:10–11 tells us to be strong and to stand: "Finally, be strong in the Lord and in his mighty power. Put on the full armor of God so that you can take your stand against the devil's schemes." It's a rumble we can win, but not with our own muscle. Victory is only in the power of Christ.

So sometimes we're instructed to flee. Sometimes stand. How do we know when to stand and when to run? We study God's Word, our truest of every "whatever is true," and we allow his Holy Spirit to give us all the right cues. Proverbs 3:5–6 tells us to trust the Lord to direct us—and he will:

> Lean on, trust in, and be confident in the Lord with all your heart and mind and do not rely on your own insight or understanding. In

all your ways know, recognize, and acknowledge Him, and He will direct and make straight and plain your paths.

AMP

The Choice Is Ours

To live lives of peace and victory, we must decide whether we'll base our life on God's priorities or the priorities of our flesh and the world's way of thinking. The two mind-sets are totally incompatible. And we choose. Will we accept godless teachings and let them become part of our thinking, or will we flee, stand, or fight?

Before you came to Christ, there was no choice to make. You lived your life according to the flesh—grabbing for whatever your flesh desired. The world and our culture feed that kind of thinking, working to convince us that we need to satisfy ourselves and that we're each, in essence, the "god" of our own little world.

But since you've given your life to Jesus, the opposite is true. His command is to have God's desires as your top priority and your own desires at the bottom of the list. We've been instructed to deny ourselves, pick up our crosses every day, and follow Christ. As a matter of fact, you know that you're growing in Christ and growing in holy living when you find yourself less focused on fleshly wants and less attracted to the sinful acts the world tells us will satisfy. You find yourself, instead, desiring to become more and more like Christ. You find your old sinful habits being replaced with new habits of holiness. And you find those old habits leaving a bad taste in your mouth as you see yourself instead wanting more and more of him.

Accessorizing Our Robes of Righteousness

There's real peace in recognizing the best, most essential accessories of life. They're undeniably un-meltable. How do I want to be dressed when I stand before God? In the shining righteousness of Christ, in the blinging beauty of Jesus. How many are going to rely on their own righteousness? Isaiah 64:6 tells us that "all our righteous acts are like filthy rags." We have nothing without him.

Can you imagine standing before the creator of all there is, thinking you look pretty classy, only to look down and find you're wearing rotten, stinking rags? It would be ever so much worse than standing there in melted accessories.

Real peace comes when we understand that we don't have to work to make ourselves bling. The shining, glorious beauty of the righteousness of Jesus takes away any fear of rejection or of not measuring up. He is our peace. "Christ himself is our peace. . . . Yes, it is through Christ we all have the right to come to the Father in one Spirit" (Eph. 2:14, 18 NCV). We can stand before him confidently with Jesus as our peace.

Running Toward Peace

Standing when we're supposed to stand and running when we're supposed to run. It's great to do the right thing at the right time. And knowing that we'll be standing before him clothed in the righteousness of Christ instead of depending on our own version of righteousness will bring us sweet peace. Run away from unholiness and into sweet peace!

And for your summer reference, the right thing to do when you see a hummingbird in the yard is to run. Especially if you don't have a saddle. I've heard they're difficult to tame.

God's solid foundation stands firm, sealed with this inscription: "The Lord knows those who are his," and, "Everyone who confesses the name of the Lord must turn away from wickedness." In a large house there are articles not only of gold and silver, but also of wood and clay; some are for noble purposes and some for ignoble. If a man cleanses himself from the latter, he will be an instrument for noble purposes, made holy, useful to the Master and prepared to do any good work. Flee the evil desires of youth, and pursue righteousness, faith, love and peace, along with those who call on the Lord out of a pure heart.

2 Timothy 2:19–22

20 The Long and Short of a Good Necklace

Giving All, the Holy How-To's

I go to great lengths, so to speak, to wear correctly proportioned neck-bling. But how do you truly know when a necklace is exactly the right length? I can tell you from experience that it's much easier to know when a necklace is the *wrong* length. Case in point: I knew one particular necklace of mine was too long when I was walking along, and it caught on a doorknob. I all but hanged myself.

That's going to leave a mark.

The long and short of it is that sometimes it's tough to tell the long and short of it. For anyone who might need a few necklace-length guidelines, maybe you can measure against these top ten.

Top Ten Ways You Can Tell Your Necklace Is the Wrong Length

1. It looks to be about the same length as your bracelet.
2. It looks to be about the same length as *you.*
3. You put it on but immediately have to have CPR.
4. You put it on but immediately step on it and take a flying header.

5. You catch the kids using it for their Barbie dolls.
6. You catch the kids using it for a jump rope.
7. You lose it in a small pile of rubber bands.
8. You lose it but find it with a person on the other end, using it to bungee jump.
9. It came in a ring box.
10. It came in a storage unit.

The long and short of necklace lengths? Okay, that's not usually life or death—except for the occasional doorknob threat. But the long and short of holiness is that there's one way to ensure you're on the right and holy road. You make sure you've given all. That's the only correct measurement. Absolutely all.

God's Longing

You've probably guessed that I dearly love the way Andrew Murray wrote, spoke, taught, lived. He was born in the 1800s and was known for having a heart for missions and for passionately calling his listeners and readers to have a rich devotion to living the life of holiness in Christ. In *The Deeper Christian Life*, under the heading of "Consecration," he wrote:

> And your God, oh, my friends, your God, His heart, His Father's heart of love, longs, longs, longs to have you give Him everything. It is not a demand. It is a demand, but it is not a demand of a hard Master, it is the call of a loving Father, who knows that every gift you bring to God will bind you closer to Himself, and every surrender you make will open your heart wider to get more of his spiritual gifts. Oh, friends! A gift to God has in His sight infinite value. It delights Him. He sees of the travail of His soul and is satisfied. And it brings unspeakable blessing to you.[1]

God is long on . . . well . . . longing. Just as Andrew Murray writes, God the Father truly does long to have you give him everything. Isn't it amazing to think that in our every surrender to him, we understand more of him and we're able to receive more of him. More blessing. More of the holy life. More peace. More him!

The Holy How

If we boil holiness down to the simplest how-to's, that's what we have: more him. We need reminders all along the road to holiness that we can't become holy on our own. We can do our part to invite holy living. But waving a wand and making ourselves holy is just not in our power.

The temple in the Old Testament was a holy place. But what was it that made the temple holy? It wasn't the long or the short of it—the measurements—though they were very specific. It was the fact that the holy God chose to dwell there. And that's exactly what makes us holy. The holy God chooses to dwell in us by his Spirit. We can invite him in, in all his holiness. First Corinthians 3:16 says, "Don't you know that you yourselves are God's temple and that God's Spirit lives in you?"

How incomparably wonderful it is that he desires to live in us. Is keeping your mind on holy things your desire? Is living a life of holiness your heart's longing? Give him your everything—your all. The up and the down, the long and the short. All. Invite him into your life. Welcome him in. By giving your all, you're indicating that you want to become like him, to live out his kind of holiness. Tell him that living for him in holiness is your greatest desire and make it part of your every thought.

Marked for Real Life

According to 1 Thessalonians 5:23–24, it's the God of peace who makes us holy: "Now may the God of peace make you holy in every way, and may your whole spirit and soul and body be kept blameless until our Lord Jesus Christ comes again. God will make this happen, for he who calls you is faithful" (NLT[b]). He is faithful and has all power to make you holy through and through. And guess what marks the life of the person whose mind is focused on allowing him to bring holiness? Peace!

Holy living and peace. Now that's going to leave a mark.

As a follower of the Lord, I order you to stop living like stupid, god-less people. Their minds are in the dark, and they are stubborn and ignorant and have missed out on the life that comes from God. They no longer have any feelings about what is right, and they are so greedy that they do all kinds of indecent things. But that isn't what you were taught about Jesus Christ. He is the truth, and you heard about him and learned about him. You were told that your foolish desires will destroy you and that you must give up your old way of life with all its bad habits. Let the Spirit change your way of thinking and make you into a new person. You were created to be like God, and so you must please him and be truly holy.

Ephesians 4:17–24 CEV

PART 5

"KEEP YOUR MINDS ON WHATEVER IS . . . FRIENDLY AND PROPER"

ACCESSORY 21
TO THE CRIME

Seeing through His Eyes

I had five babies in seven years. I fondly call most of that first decade the barf years. For the most part, I accessorized during those years with baby scum of varying consistencies and occasionally with gum someone accidentally stuck in my hair. Instead of blinging with rings and things, I often wore a pacifier around one finger, a barf towel over each shoulder, and usually had a trail of dried, glimmering apple juice down one side. My mom-accessories were right out there for everyone to see. If it was a fashion crime, would that make all my embellishments accessories to the crime? Or maybe accessories to the grime. I wonder why it never occurred to me to just wear Teflon.

Two of my five children are girls. That means that as they got a little older, we got to step up the accessorizing a bit. I soon noticed them developing their own tastes in jewelry. And I do mean "tastes," because by the time they were four or five, most of their accessories were edible. Sweet-Tart necklaces. Gummy bracelets. Ring Pops. Wear them, then eat them. Personally I could never quite get into the edible accessories. It's hard to justify buying an outfit to coordinate with any piece of jewelry you later plan to ingest.

Tasty Insights

Now my girls are teens. Accessory needs have changed. And they've risen in price, I might add. But I've noticed my teens have new insights these days that are not only jewelry related. Teenagers know a lot more about some things than we give them credit for.

My daughter Kaley was telling me recently, for instance, that if you want to know how much people truly like you, approach them when they have a bag of Skittles. If they don't readily offer to fork over a Skittle or two, no real love there. If they offer, but they're the kind of friends who pour them into their own hand first, then pick you out a yellow or a green one, still pretty surfacey, wimpy kind of love.

If it's a real, genuine, unselfish love, they'll give you a handful. And not just any random handful. Nosiree. They'll make sure you get plenty of reds and purples. That's love, man.

We're instructed in this portion of Philippians 4:8 to keep on thinking about whatever is "friendly and proper." "Friendly" speaks of kindness and graciousness, behaving to others in a way that's pleasing and full of love. "Proper" refers to doing things for others that would cause a person to be well-thought-of or well-regarded, showing courtesy and respect for others.

The Color of Love

Our goal should be to love people in the friendliest and most proper way—in the biggest taste of the rainbow. Loving with kindness and graciousness and with courtesy and respect means loving all the way to the reds and purples.

First Peter 3:8–9 gives us instruction in the tastiest red and purple love when it says,

> Finally, all of you should be of one mind, full of sympathy toward each other, loving one another with tender hearts and humble minds.

Don't repay evil for evil. Don't retaliate when people say unkind things about you. Instead, pay them back with a blessing. That is what God wants you to do, and he will bless you for it.

NLT^a

When we show that mature kind of love to each other—the agreeable, sympathetic, tenderhearted, humble, forgiving, blessing kind of love—according to this passage, we're doing exactly what God the Father wants us to do. And he blesses us for it! Our relationships are blessed as well.

It only makes sense that we'll never experience a truly peaceful life if we neglect to do our part to have this kind of blessed peace with others. And it's our blessed calling.

Hospitality You Can See

Scripture spells it out plainly that we're called to be hospitable. And we are called to be hospitable not just to show off how good we are at . . . well . . . being hospitable. First Peter 4:8–9 says, "Above all, love each other deeply, because love covers over a multitude of sins. Offer hospitality to one another without grumbling." We're to show an active love, kindness, and hospitality to others not just to impress them but to serve in humility.

In Luke 7:36–50 we're told about a Pharisee who invited Jesus to come to his home. I imagine Simon was known as one great host, a party guy who knew how to put together a nice soirée. How he must've wanted to impress Jesus—and any onlookers too, since in their culture they opened up their better parties for outsiders to watch.

Can you imagine what was going through Simon's mind as he finally got this up-and-coming rabbi, Jesus, to come to his party of the season, and who crashes the gala? None other than some goes-to-all-the-wrong-kind-of-parties gal. And it's one thing to nonchalantly crash a party. But no. This gal had to make a scene. A big one.

Weeping, lowering herself to stand behind Jesus, sobbing all over him, washing his feet with her tears and her hair. A totally low-class act at his uptown-wannabe party.

See This?

Jesus knew that Simon was appalled at the fact that Jesus let this woman of ill repute touch him. He told Simon a story of forgiveness, then asked Simon, "Do you see this woman?"

See her? How could he miss her? She was the object of everyone's attention, much to Simon's chagrin. But it's one thing to see, and another to really *see*. Simon was more focused on her as the immoral party wrecker. He wanted to impress Jesus instead of love Jesus as the woman did. Simon wanted to show others what a grand party-guy he was, instead of lowering himself to serve. He was all about his rep and the party crasher hardly deserved his attention, in his eyes.

But Jesus looked with different eyes. He was more impressed with the sinful woman than he was with Simon. She was a woman who knew what it meant to desire repentance and forgiveness with everything she had. And while Simon missed what she was really about, Jesus saw her—truly *saw* her.

Making a Blacklist and Checking It Twice

Are there people we need to *see?* Do we knowingly or unknowingly blacklist the unlovely? And think about it. Do you allow Jesus to *see* the real you?

I mentioned, didn't I, that sometimes our kids know a lot more about how people should be treated than we give them credit for? My oldest son is a young musician. That Andy Rhea continually comes up with lyrics that bless me straight to the heart with their deep insight. He wrote a song called "Seeing Through Your Eyes" that's very up front about not always seeing clearly.

"Seeing Through Your Eyes"

by Andy Rhea

I've been using your eyes
To help me see all I've missed
I'm tired of being unwise
I'm squinting through miles of mist
To find your porch again, my Love
To find the where and when you were thinking of

Love will let me see
And your life has set me free from me

Now I am seeing new shapes
With wild, unseen, vibrant hues
They're pointing far from death's wake
They're leading me straight to you
And now the lights are on in living tones
And now I'm finally free to call this home

Love will let me see
And your life has set me free
And I will not refrain
From saying, "Redeemed is my new name"[1]

As we learn to look more through Jesus's eyes, he opens our eyes to see others clearly. In Andrew's words, "Love will let me see."

God's loving gift of salvation sets us free to be who we were meant to be. And it's at the point we become who we're meant to be—finally feeling at home in our own skin—that he can use us to share our "new name" with those around us, by our testimony and by the way we love them in kindness and graciousness—by the way we find ourselves genuinely *seeing* them.

Eyes Wide Open

The last recorded words of Jesus to the sinful woman who anointed his feet and washed them with her tears were "Go in peace" (Luke 7:50).

What a gift! With an eyes-wide-open love comes a heart-wide-open peace.

Don't you adore how love and peace are packaged so perfectly together? They're even better together than motherhood and Teflon.

Now one of the Pharisees invited Jesus to have dinner with him, so he went to the Pharisee's house and reclined at the table. When a woman who had lived a sinful life in that town learned that Jesus was eating at the Pharisee's house, she brought an alabaster jar of perfume, and as she stood behind him at his feet weeping, she began to wet his feet with her tears. Then she wiped them with her hair, kissed them and poured perfume on them.

When the Pharisee who had invited him saw this, he said to himself, "If this man were a prophet, he would know who is touching him and what kind of woman she is—that she is a sinner."

Jesus answered him, "Simon, I have something to tell you."

"Tell me, teacher," he said.

"Two men owed money to a certain moneylender. One owed him five hundred denarii, and the other fifty. Neither of them had the money to pay him back, so he canceled the debts of both. Now which of them will love him more?"

Simon replied, "I suppose the one who had the bigger debt canceled."

"You have judged correctly," Jesus said.

Then he turned toward the woman and said to Simon, "Do you see this woman? I came into your house. You did not give me any water for my feet, but she wet my feet with her tears and wiped them with her hair. You did not give me a kiss, but this woman, from the time I entered, has not stopped kissing my feet. You did not put oil on my head, but she has poured perfume on my feet. Therefore, I tell you, her many sins have been forgiven—for she loved much. But he who has been forgiven little loves little."

Then Jesus said to her, "Your sins are forgiven."

The other guests began to say among themselves, "Who is this who even forgives sins?"

Jesus said to the woman, "Your faith has saved you; go in peace."

Luke 7:36–50

BLING IT ON 22

Kindness/Serving Others/Giving

Why doesn't anyone make accessories for thighs? Now there's a place I could use some clever camouflage and magical misdirection. As it is, no magic: now you see them, now you still see them. In duplicate.

Thigh-rings? Thigh-laces? Thigh-lets? I'm not sure what thigh jewelry would be called, but I know exactly what its job would be: draw all attention away from the thighs themselves. Not only are these thighs heavier than I'd like, they look like they've suffered some major hail damage.

Heavy Sighs, Heavy Thighs

I'm convincing myself more by the second that there could actually be a market for thigh-bling.

I had a heavy reminder of the thigh situation the other day. I had to get a physical for insurance purposes. Incidentally, isn't it a little ironic that they take a quart or two of blood, then tell you you're borderline anemic? It's nice that they'll give you that personal touch and come right to your home. But then they get a little more personal and ask every question in this health universe and the next.

And would you believe that on top of the pokes and the gazillion questions, that smarty little nurse girl made me *weigh in*? That was past personal and downright merciless. Adding weight-insult to poke-injury, she even brought her own scale! It was like she thought I was going to cheat, for Pete's sake. Hey, if I had planned to cheat, I would've started with my date of birth.

No Weigh, Man

To further the exasperation, her scale was obviously out of calibration. Way out. I stepped on, looked down at the number, then looked behind me to see if smarty-nurse had gotten on there with me.

Okay, she wasn't on the scale. But I started to seriously question her credentials about that time. Surely no legitimate health care professional would give a person a weight number like that without a crash cart handy. Some antidepressants, at the very least.

This is all pretty personal, but let me just tell you that this is not a good way to get a good rate on a new insurance policy. You wouldn't believe the premium they quoted. Ouch. Since it didn't seem to work in my favor anyway, I've decided that at any future physicals, I don't care what the nurse has in that big black bag. We're doing the weighing on *my* scale.

And also for the record, it seems those traveling nurses don't all respond well to asking if you can weigh one thigh at a time. It's all in. Ouch again.

Give 'til It Hurts?

While we're getting personal, I think sometimes we make certain issues painful when they're really not. Giving, for instance. Not paying premiums, but real giving. And not just giving what's expected, but going radically beyond. Do you know what Jesus said about giving? In Luke 6:38 he said, "Give, and it will be given to you. A good measure, pressed down, shaken together and running over, will be poured into your lap. For with the measure you use, it will be measured to you."

Those words are painful when we're falling short. But they're so exciting when we're generously giving. Not that we should ever give just to receive a blessing, but the thought of blessings that can't be measured is still thrilling. Overflowing blessings! No scales can measure them. Only in this context, it's a good thing. A very good thing.

Giving to Jesus through our tithes and offerings and giving to him by being generous to his people is a blessed way to live. When we keep our minds on things that are friendly and proper, giving is a natural expression of that mind-set. And giving our service fits right in. Giving and *doing*.

Bling, Blang, Blung

I know I've used "bling" as a verb several dozen times already. Is that even grammatically legal? Can *bling* be a verb?

Either way, there's nothing illegal about putting a little extra "verb" in keeping our minds on whatever is friendly and proper. Giving and serving—those are things we need to *do*. It's a doing that invites peace into our lives.

Peace is God's will for your life. And peace is our calling. We've looked at Colossians 3:15 and its instruction to let the peace of Christ rule in our hearts, but notice too that the last part of the verse says, "Since as members of one body you were called to peace." Peace is not just a hope or a desire or a wish. It's a calling. When you're called into a ministry, you study, you train, you pray, you work, and grow. It's much the same with his calling of peace on our lives. As we keep our focus on him, and as we keep our noses in his Word, we learn more and more how to let him rule and how to let his rule impact our relationships with each other as we live out his call to peace.

Grow in the Call

Growing in our calling to give to and to serve others may take some work. Sometimes we're called to sacrifice our own desires. Sometimes we're called to give and serve even when we don't feel like it.

In 2 Samuel 18–19, David was in deep despair over the death of his son, Absalom. Second Samuel 18:33 says, "Then the king was deeply moved, and went up to the chamber over the gate, and wept. And as he went, he said thus: 'O my son Absalom—my son, my son Absalom—if only I had died in your place!" (NKJV). This was serious heartbreak. But even though David's heart was broken, he had to put his grief aside for the sake of his people. Joab told him that his people needed comfort, and David received Joab's counsel and humbly responded. Second Samuel 19:8 says, "Then the king arose and sat in the gate." Going to the gate represented his return to his duties as king.

Have you ever had to put aside your own feelings of despair or grief or pain to meet someone else's need? Every time you become willing to sacrifice your own needs to meet the needs of others in obedience to God, your Father meets your every need. When you have no strength, he will be your strength, just as when you need wisdom, he will be your wisdom.

James 3:17–18 says,

> Real wisdom, God's wisdom, begins with a holy life and is characterized by getting along with others. It is gentle and reasonable, overflowing with mercy and blessings, not hot one day and cold the next, not two-faced. You can develop a healthy, robust community that lives right with God and enjoy its results only if you do the hard work of getting along with each other, treating each other with dignity and honor.
>
> Message

Joining in the struggle of a friend in need, taking up the cause to pray for her, is a loving and giving act. Romans 15:30 says, "I urge you, brothers, by our Lord Jesus Christ and by the love of the Spirit, to join me in my struggle by praying to God for me."

I don't want to be the kind of friend who says, "Sure, I'll pray for you," then forgets as soon as the friend is out of sight. Sometimes being a good friend is sacrificing time and energy and coming along-side to truly join in her struggle.

Verb On!

Giving, serving, sacrificing, and praying for people in the friendly, proper way is about what we think and what we *do*. As the Lord leads, are you ready to put a little more "do" in your service? Ready to *verb* it?

Okay, so now I'm using *verb* as a verb. Someone needs to stop me.

> Remember this: Whoever sows sparingly will also reap sparingly, and whoever sows generously will also reap generously. Each man should give what he has decided in his heart to give, not reluctantly or under compulsion, for God loves a cheerful giver. And God is able to make all grace abound to you, so that in all things at all times, having all that you need, you will abound in every good work.
>
> 2 Corinthians 9:6–8

ON PEARLS 23 AND SWINE

Relationship Difficulties/Bitterness

June Cleaver always seemed to wear her pearls, didn't she? They were a little like her name tag. There was something particularly classy about a strand of pearls during that era. And between the pearls and the white, starched-like-titanium apron, June brought a definite sophistication to the well-accessorized working-at-home woman.

There is one thing that puzzles me, though. Ward and June seemed to be the epitome of sophistication and put the "class" in middle class in the '50s and '60s. So I can't imagine the following conversation happening. On the other hand, somewhere in the background story, it must've happened.

Ward and June in the Hospital Maternity Ward, Just After Delivery

"Ward, I simply can't agree to it."

"Come on, June. It'll be funny."

"Get serious, dear. How could we expect the boy to succeed with that kind of label?"

"I think you're reading entirely too much into it, dear."

"Sure, Ward. Then why don't we just call him 'Weasel'? Can you imagine trying to have a serious conversation someday with 'The Wease'?"

"Actually, that does have a ring to it, June dear. I hadn't considered that one."

"Oh honestly, Ward. And I suppose 'Warthog' or 'Turkey' or 'Pig' or 'Muskrat' or 'Gopher' would make you happy too? Maybe we could throw in some spider monkeys and an elephant or two, and we could have an entire zoo!"

"Hmm, let me try that last one on. 'Look, Baby Wally. This is your new brother, 'The Goph.' Yes, good one, June."

"Oh for Pete's sake, Ward. Fine, let's just stick with 'The Beaver'—though how you get 'Beaver' from 'Theodore' is beyond me. At least I won our last argument like this one. Otherwise we'd be introducing the new baby to his big brother, 'The Possum.'"

Muskrat Love

What's in a name? Probably not so much. After all, America would've fallen in love with the Beaver no matter which animal label they'd given him.

Whatever we call them, it is important to have godly people we name as our friends. Do you have people who are close to you, those you name as friends? Life can be trying. Let me encourage you not to "try" it all by yourself. There's no way we can follow the instruction to operate in "friendly and proper" mode without being involved with people.

You may be thinking right now that relationships can be a real headache. And I have to admit you'd be right in thinking it. Larry

Mondello and Eddie Haskell pop to mind. To have peace in our relationships, we have to be willing to work at that peace, to pursue it: *"Therefore let us pursue the things which make for peace and the things by which one may edify another" (Rom. 14:19 NKJV).*

Just as sure as relationships require work, we desperately need those relationships. From the very beginning it was obvious that God didn't design us to go it alone.

Label Us Workers

So much of Scripture deals with relationships. That tells us two things. The first is that relationships are important to the Lord. The second is that they require a lot of instruction, reminders, more instruction . . . *work.*

Are you working to reach out to people? Are you actively offering friendship? It often requires a willingness to step out of your comfort zone. And at some point or another, it always requires a willingness to serve, to put another person's needs and desires ahead of your own. If you're experiencing a bit of a lean friendship season, don't sit back and wait for someone else to reach out to you. Make the first move. Proverbs 18:24 says, "A man who has friends must himself be friendly, but there is a friend who sticks closer than a brother" (NKJV). Label yourself friendly.

Casting Your Pearls before Swine?

What do you do when you've gone the extra mile to label yourself friendly, but your friend responds by being a jerk to you? Excuse me for saying so, but sometimes even the best of people can be real swine. Here's a handful of points to consider:

- Decide if it's a sin issue (the kind you need to lovingly confront).
- Decide if it's a weakness (the kind you need to patiently rise above).

- If your friend has accused you, check to see if there's any truth in the accusation. Is there something the Lord might want to change in you? Let the Lord grow you through your friend's honesty, even if the honesty is a bit brutal. "Wounds from a friend can be trusted, but an enemy multiplies kisses" (Prov. 27:6).
- If your friend has accused you but the accusations were born out of your friend's misunderstandings, jealousies, or other immaturities, do what you can to clear up the problem and restore the relationship. It's true that some friendships require more work than others.
- Remember that sometimes you're the swine.

Responding through a Filter

However you choose to respond to a wound from a friend, ask the Lord to help you exhibit the kind of love, forgiveness, wisdom, and maturity that flows out of a close, abiding relationship with him. Ask him to give you the ability to offer grace instead of your ooey-gooey flesh. Let every response be filtered through the will of God for your friend and for you. Ask God to give you the strength to bless instead of hurling an insult right back. That's how Jesus responded. And it becomes our blessing when we choose to respond like him, in the power of his Holy Spirit.

It's true that we're sometimes called to serve people who rub us the wrong way. Are you dealing with a difficult person, thinking surely Jesus doesn't expect you to serve *her?* Think about this. In the humility act of all humility acts, Jesus washed twelve pairs of dirty disciple-feet, perhaps scrubbing between all 120 disciple toes. Remember that ten of those toes belonged to Judas, the betrayer. Jesus washed Judas's feet too, knowing who he was and what he would do! *O Lord, give us the strength of character and the love and forgiveness needed to wash the feet of others.*

Since we mentioned forgiveness, let me tuck in a reminder to get rid of any speck of bitterness. Even the tiniest seed can take root. And what an ugly mess grows from there! Label it nasty. In Colossians 3:13 we're told to "bear with each other and forgive whatever grievances you may have against one another. Forgive as the Lord forgave you."

Bitterness is peace poison. And it spreads. It can begin in one relationship, but then affects every relationship. It can poison your entire family and on into future generations. Please don't underestimate the destructive power of unforgiveness.

Ready, Set, Forgive

If there's someone you haven't forgiven, will you choose by faith to forgive? Is there a face that pops into your mind every time you hear or read the word "bitterness"? That could be an indication that the poison is creeping into your life. Don't let it kill your fruitfulness and your joy—and the joy of your family and friends. Choose to forgive. Forgive in the Colossians 3:13 way: "as the Lord forgave you." In the light of all he's forgiven us, how can we not forgive?

By the way, forgiving doesn't mean you're saying that someone who hurt you is not responsible. It's not saying that what that person did was okay or that it's excused. It's choosing in the grace of God not to hold it against them, letting go of hate.

You may be thinking that you tried forgiveness and couldn't really get it to take. You said the words "I forgive," but five minutes later the bitterness was back. Sometimes forgiveness happens instantly. I love it when God works that way in a heart. Sometimes, though, he wants you to depend on him moment by moment for that forgiveness. Sometimes you have to say, "Lord, by faith right now I forgive this person." Then you may have to do it again in an hour. You may have to do it every hour. But by God's grace as you faithfully forgive, you can see an hour become a day. Then a day become a week. Pretty soon, you may just find yourself praying for that person who's hurt you, asking God to work in the lives of those who've hurt you—asking him to bless them. Label them forgiven! I'm telling you, we have a God just that big!

If you've been longing for peace but haven't been able to truly make it your own, this area of forgiveness could be your door to experiencing the incomparable, unexplainable, totally remarkable peace of God. Forgiveness will renew your life and give you peace you're hardly going to be able to believe!

Don't Weasel Out

We honor God when we freely offer friendship. To be obedient and to experience his peace, there's no other choice. So let me encourage you not to try to weasel out of being a good friend, offering love, service, and forgiveness. There is great peace and blessing there.

And no, I promise I'm not calling you "Weasel."

> Two are better than one,
>> because they have a good return for their work:
> If one falls down,
>> his friend can help him up.
>> But pity the man who falls
>> and has no one to help him up!
> Also, if two lie down together, they will keep warm.
>> But how can one keep warm alone?
> Though one may be overpowered,
>> two can defend themselves.
>> A cord of three strands is not quickly broken.
>
> Ecclesiastes 4:9–12

Silver Lining 24

When Someone Refuses Friendship,
Peace at Any Cost?

Surprise jewelry—always fun! And don't you love being at a restaurant when some guy pops the question to an unsuspecting girlfriend? Who doesn't love to see the trembling fellow pulling an engagement ring from somewhere clever while his girl squeals and cries?

Those are the sweet surprises. And then there are the surprises that are not so sweet.

I was teaching at a women's event and at one point the ladies were asked to share a surprise moment in their lives. One shared about a night she was out with friends for a big event. They were all bling-bedecked in their most sparkly finery. Just before heading in for the dinner portion of the evening, she reached into her purse for her lip liner and put on a nice fresh layer.

The second she made her entrance and started toward the dinner table, her friends all but tackled her. They were laughing hysterically and asking what in the world she had done. Boy, was she confused. One of her friends pulled a little mirror from her purse and handed it to her and when she looked into it, she actually scared herself. She had accidentally pulled out her black eyeliner instead of her lip pencil. Surprise! She looked like one of the living dead from some horror flick.

Every lip does not necessarily have a silver lining. Makeup and accessory surprises on the whole can be challenging. The top ten bad accessory surprises in this list, for instance.

Top Ten Bad Accessory Surprises

1. You're meeting friends for lunch, pull out your glasses to read the menu, then realize they're your husband's.
2. You take off your new hat and a bunny pops out.
3. Your new bracelet is lovingly engraved, "To Sally, With Love Forever," but your name is not Sally.
4. The precious stone in your new jewelry piece turns out to be just a stone.
5. Your lovely new ankle bracelet is actually a prisoner tracking device.
6. You find something suspicious in your locket and later discover that it's microfilm containing plans to overthrow a small government.
7. Your fox scarf turns out to be an actual fox—you know, a live one.
8. You find out your new bracelet is magnetic when you suddenly notice your wrist is stuck to your left earring.
9. The first time you turn off the lights, you discover that your new ring glows in the dark.
10. Your sweetheart finally pops the question, but that new hunk of ice actually melts.

Fully Engaged

What happens when you've fully engaged, so to speak, in investing yourself in everything "friendly and proper," but someone refuses your friendliness? Our Father does want us to have relationships that are peaceful. But he also understands people and their failings and inadequacies. It never catches him off guard when someone doesn't respond to your offer of friendship. He's not even surprised when there are people who just refuse to get along with you altogether. And while it's his desire that we all live in peace, he has never locked us in to pursuing peace at any price.

I do believe he's called us to go the extra mile. And then maybe even another mile or two. We're given scriptural guidelines for forgiving not just once, but forgiving again and again. God has gone to great lengths to encourage us to have self-sacrificing attitudes toward others and to show compassion, forgiveness, mercy, and grace. But there are times after we've gone that extra mile or two that we understand that, despite our most gung-ho try, peace is not possible. That's a for-sure when peace with an individual is only possible through violation of a scriptural principle.

We're never, ever called to compromise the commands of God to have peace with an individual. James 3:17 says, "But the wisdom from above is first pure, then peaceable" (NKJV). We should never seek peace at the expense of purity. Peace comes *through* purity—and purity comes first.

Peace as Far as Possible

Romans 12:18 says, "If it is possible, as far as it depends on you, live at peace with everyone." But you're only responsible for your own actions, "as far as it depends on you."

We're called to be friendly and proper to everyone, but we're also cautioned in Scripture to choose our best, closest buds wisely and carefully. Proverbs 22:24–25 says, for instance, "Don't befriend angry people or associate with hot-tempered people, or you will learn to be like them and endanger your soul" (NLT[b]). We're to avoid those toxic kinds of relationships that will drag us down. In Psalm 129:4, David rejoiced when it was God himself who set him free from destructive relationships: "But the LORD is good; he has cut me free from the ropes of the ungodly" (NLT[b]).

Isn't it true that ungodly people actually can tangle us up in their ropes of manipulation, lies, sinful habits, and in their desire to get us to go in their own destructive direction? If you see yourself getting roped into a relationship you know will not promote your spiritual health or growth, ask the Lord himself to snip those ropes. Ask him and he will free you. He can give you the power—and he can send godly people to come alongside you and help you when you're about to get entangled. Ask and he will answer.

Set Some Boundaries

Often those toxic kind of people are family members or co-workers, people we can't logically avoid. But we can be kind and gracious, yet still keep a reasonable distance. Scripture gives us cause to set wise boundaries with certain people. Whether we want to or not, we so often become like those we hang out with on a regular basis.

If you've confided in a friend who betrayed that confidence, freely forgive, but understand that you have reason to set new boundaries in that friendship. Proverbs 11:13 says, "A talebearer reveals secrets, but he who is of a faithful spirit conceals a matter" (NKJV).

It's okay to have specific boundaries for specific friends. Your closest friends should be those who are obediently following Christ and growing in wisdom. Proverbs 11:22 says, "As a ring of gold in a swine's snout, so is a lovely woman who lacks discretion" (NKJV). What a waste of gold! Have a different set of "don't go there" borders for the friend who isn't well-accessorized in the wisdom of God, than the borders you have for those you know actively and passionately follow Christ. You need to make sure that if you spend time with that kind of friend, you're the one having an influence on her, not the other way around.

Hanging In There, Endeavoring

We have a bond with believers—and would you believe that the bond is all wrapped up in the peace of God? Ephesians 4:3 says, "Endeavoring to keep the unity of the Spirit in the bond of peace" (NKJV). We certainly should never take that "endeavoring" lightly. Hebrews 12:14 says, "Work at living in peace with everyone, and work at living a holy life."

Working at peace and working at living a holy life. Two life accessories that go together like love and marriage. Love and marriage and a ring that doesn't melt.

> Love must be sincere. Hate what is evil; cling to what is good. Be devoted to one another in brotherly love. Honor one another above yourselves. Never be lacking in zeal, but keep your spiritual fervor, serving the Lord. Be joyful in hope, patient in affliction, faithful in prayer. Share with God's people who are in need. Practice hospitality.
>
> Bless those who persecute you; bless and do not curse. Rejoice with those who rejoice; mourn with those who mourn. Live in harmony with one another. Do not be proud, but be willing to associate with people of low position. Do not be conceited.
>
> Do not repay anyone evil for evil. Be careful to do what is right in the eyes of everybody. If it is possible, as far as it depends on you, live at peace with everyone. Do not take revenge, my friends, but leave room for God's wrath, for it is written: "It is mine to avenge; I will repay," says the Lord. On the contrary:
>
> "If your enemy is hungry, feed him;
>
> if he is thirsty, give him something to drink.
>
> In doing this, you will heap burning coals on his head." Do not be overcome by evil, but overcome evil with good.
>
> Romans 12:9–21

DO YOUR EARS 25 HANG LOW?

Our Words

Friends are there for each other in every accessory need. A good friend will lend you the necklace that goes with your favorite top.

She'll make sure your husband knows which ring you want for your birthday. A good friend will keep track, then tell you when that bracelet you've had your eye on is going on sale.

There is accessory friendship that even goes beyond all that. The closest friend will tell you that the earrings you're wearing are too heavy for your earlobes. Or maybe that your lobes are too gooshy for your earrings. Either way, she'll help you guard against earlobes that look like they're touching your shoulders. Of course, if she's of a sturdier lobe constitution, she may want you to give the earrings to her. But still, it's a real friend who will tell you that your ears are hanging too low, wobbling to and fro. Sometimes being a good friend means saying something that's a little difficult to say.

Other times, being a good friend means saying nothing at all. My friend Peanuts recently witnessed one of the finest friendship moments I think I've ever heard of. It was at a hair salon. One of the stylists was washing the hair of her client/friend. The friend was lying back with her head in the washbowl and the two were chitchatting in a friendly manner as the stylist leaned over her.

One little word formed just the wrong way caused a rather tragic happenstance—the stylist lost control of her chewing gum. That wouldn't have been so bad, except that it fell right out of her mouth. That wouldn't have been so bad either, except that . . . *it fell right smack-dab into the open mouth of her client!* No kidding. Ga-ross!

Thanks, but No Thanks

Peanuts watched quietly. Okay, she watched relatively quietly while she fought off the urge to scream-laugh, point, then roll hysterically on the floor. But she held it all in to see what in the world the secondhand-gum-chewing client would do.

In all honesty, that poor woman with her head in her hair gal's washbowl could've *patooey*ed the alien gum right back out at her friend. She could've spat and sputtered and made a big scene, and she would've been fairly justified. But what did she do? She calmly reached her hand from under the cape, took the gum out of her own mouth, and handed it back to her friend.

I'd like to imagine her saying something like, "No thanks, I usually go for spearmint." But she didn't. And her unruffled stylist friend simply tossed it in the wastebasket. Neither of them mentioned it! Isn't that hilarious? It didn't even interrupt their conversation! Now that's friendship!

Chew on This

One little word formed just the wrong way can lead to more than gum troubles. As we're seeking to keep our minds on things that are friendly and proper, our words are oh so important. Proverbs 10:20 says, "The tongue of the righteous is choice silver; the heart of the wicked is worth little" (NKJV). Choice silver we understand! The psalmist is talking accessory language. He's reminding us that good words are valuable. They're precious.

It can be so easy to give in to negative words about difficult people. It's easy to slip into patterns of gossip, to exaggerate one "truth" while minimizing another and to let the unkind remarks fly. Very easy to do. And anything but silver-coated.

We looked at 1 Peter 3:10–11 in chapter 18. It clearly connects our words and our peace pursuit: "For whoever would love life and see good days must keep his tongue from evil and his lips from deceitful speech. He must turn from evil and do good; he must seek peace and pursue it." Using our words in hurtful or deceitful ways is evil use of our tongues—and it tears down our churches, our families, and our own personal lives. It's completely opposed to peace.

Word Qs

Ephesians 4:29 says, "When you talk, do not say harmful things, but say what people need—words that will help others become stronger. Then what you say will do good to those who listen to you" (NCV).

How much different our words would be if we asked ourselves a few questions based on the last two passages before we let them slip out:

- Is there anything even remotely evil in these words?
- Is there anything with even a hint of deceit or exaggeration in these words?
- Are these words of peace?
- Will these words be harmful to the one hearing them?
- Will these words be harmful to anyone else?
- Are these words that someone needs?
- Are these words that will help others become stronger?
- Will these words actively do good to those listening?
- Are these words that will bless God?
- Would I be embarrassed if I realized God is listening?

He *is* listening, you know.

Listen to This

We need to be careful what we let slip out of our mouths. We have the power to give joy, health, gladness, sweetness, and goodness to another through our words. Or the opposite. Take a look at these. They're just a little taste of the word-related Proverbs:

> Reckless words pierce like a sword, but the tongue of the wise brings healing.
>
> Proverbs 12:18

> Anxiety in the heart of man causes depression, but a good word makes it glad.
>
> Proverbs 12:25 NKJV

A gentle answer deflects anger, but harsh words make tempers flare.

The tongue of the wise makes knowledge appealing, but the mouth of a fool belches out foolishness.

Proverbs 15:1–2 NLT[b]

A man has joy in making an apt answer, and a word spoken at the right moment—how good it is!

Proverbs 15:23 AMP

Pleasant words are like a honeycomb, sweetness to the soul and health to the bones.

Proverbs 16:24 NKJV

A word aptly spoken is like apples of gold in settings of silver.

Proverbs 25:11

We have some major word power! If we worked to make sure our words promoted only good, how much different would our home be? Our church? Our workplace? What sneaky negative words do we allow to steal our peace on an average day? How often do we wake up frustrated about one thing, critical about another? Have you ever found yourself angry about your weight, but snapping at your husband instead? Have you ever found yourself frustrated at your overflowing to-do list, but being critical to your co-workers instead? How much more peace would we be experiencing if we allowed the love of Jesus to "silver-ize" our words?

Ready for the Silver Exchange?

To change our words, we have to look at our hearts. Jesus said, "The mouth speaks from the overflow of the heart" (Matt. 12:34 HCSB). Ask the Lord to reveal to you anything in your heart that might be adversely affecting your words. Ask him to reveal to you anything in your heart that needs to change, then give him full rule and reign of all of it. Ask him to give you word wisdom as you surrender your tongue to him. Proverbs 10:32 says, "The lips of the righteous know what is acceptable" (NKJV). Ask the Lord to filter your words through his righteousness.

Ask him to guard your every word, to fill your words with truth, love, wisdom, encouragement, joy, and blessing. Ask him to transform your words into words that promote peace. Ask and he will answer. It's his desire to make your words pleasing to him, pleasing to others, and you'll find they will be pleasing to you. Pleasing and fruitful.

Don't worry. These kinds of fruitful words are not related to secondhand Juicy Fruit.

> Summing up: Be agreeable, be sympathetic, be loving, be compassionate, be humble. That goes for all of you, no exceptions. No retaliation. No sharp-tongued sarcasm. Instead, bless—that's your job, to bless. You'll be a blessing and also get a blessing.
>
> 1 Peter 3:8–9 Message

PART 6

"DON'T EVER STOP THINKING ABOUT WHAT IS TRULY WORTHWHILE AND WORTHY OF PRAISE"

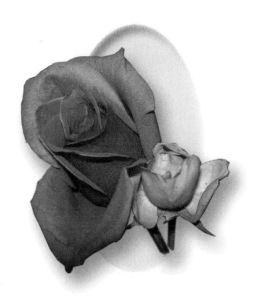

Bling-less 26
in St. Louie

Busyness

I flew out of the house one morning with my keys in one hand, my long, rather distressing to-do list in the other. The list was so long it practically fluttered behind me. It wasn't until I arrived at the post office that I realized—atrocity of atrocities—I had been so absorbed with the busyness of the day, *I forgot to accessorize!* No earrings, no necklace, no rings, no watch. Can you imagine me running all around the St. Louis area bling-naked?

Too Busy to Bling-a-tize

I have to be pretty distracted to forget to add bling. It's a busy life for all of us. My to-do list from a few weeks ago was another of those heavy-duty kinds. Anytime it takes me an entire half hour just to write out my to-do list for the day, I know it's a day I'm likely in for some hullabaloo. And that's exactly what hullaba-happened.

I probably don't need to tell you that I'm not the most organized cookie in the bag. My to-do list generally helps keep me from wasting my day flitting here and there without accomplishing the things that are most vital. So I really and truly spent half an hour building my list and numbering each item in order of importance. Okay, since organization is not my best thing, the list was on a napkin. But at least I made the list. It was a beauty. In a few hours I had a couple of items checked off with about a dozen more to go. Still overwhelming, but I was making progress.

I figured I could make faster progress if I had coffee, so I went to whip up a pot. So here's the lesson I learned that day that I'll include in my "to-do list tips" book if I ever write one: If you're going to put your to-do list on a napkin, at least make sure you put something on top of the napkin so it doesn't float off the desk. By the time I got back with my coffee, LuLu, the little dog with the Yoda ears, had run away with my list. She was under the table in the dining room. Shredding.

The Dog Ate My Homework

The next part of the hullabaloo involved an intense chase scene. I finally caught the little LuLu-fiend on one of her sideways skids and pinned her down. I fished most of the list out from under the table and a few pieces out from between her doggy molars. Man! A half hour spent on a list that was suddenly coleslaw.

LuLu was trying to look innocent. Maybe she was even trying to help me. No to-do list means nothing to do, right? Isn't a good shredding even better than a few checkmarks? And LuLu may have been thinking that if I didn't have a to-do list, I could sit around all day and toss her tennis ball, let her take a snooze in my lap, and put in some serious, all-around LuLu-pampering time. That's more of a LuLu list. Either way, the list of all the work I was trying to accomplish at home was dog chow. The dog really did eat my homework.

It was a good reminder, though, that there are times when all those things on the to-do list need to give way to the things that are most vital. It's always a good test for me when I have deadlines up to my eyebrows and I get a call from a friend who needs a listening ear. Or even when my kids want to play a game. Am I willing to shred my own agenda when the Lord might have a different one in mind? If there's something that will bring him glory that's not on my to-do list, am I willing to trade my list for his?

Whatsoever You Do

Remember, Colossians 3:2 says to "set your minds on things above, not on earthly things." Whether our temptation is to have our minds trapped in a long list of things or a long list of blings, there's an entirely different place for our minds to rest. Just a few verses later, we're given this reminder: "And whatever you do, whether in word or deed, do it all in the name of the Lord Jesus, giving thanks to God the Father through him" (v. 17).

Whether in word or deed, whether on a napkin or over the phone—or even playing tiddlywinks—I want my agenda to ever and always line up with his.

Of course, we're bound to have trouble playing tiddlywinks now. LuLu ate most of them. I think she thought they were baked beans . . . which I'm guessing she thought would go well with the coleslaw.

The list-lugging busy life really is the norm these days. But how does our busyness compare with "what is truly worthwhile and worthy of praise"?

How Busy Is Too Busy?

When do we know for sure we're too busy? When we forget the worthwhile and praiseworthy things of God—when we forget *him*. God says in Jeremiah 2:32, "Does a maiden forget her jewelry, a bride her wedding ornaments? Yet my people have forgotten me, days without number." Forgetting her jewelry? Who would do that? Okay, that hits a little close to home. But in the bigger picture, every bride wants to look her shining best for her groom, the one she adores. Our God wants us to be just as thrilled to welcome him into our day, "days without number," or "day after day."

Is there any busyness pushing your heavenly Father out of your day? There is no busyness that's more important than he is. As a matter of fact, every single item on our to-do list should be about and for him—he should always be on our minds. First Corinthians 10:31 says, "So whether you eat or drink or whatever you do, do it all for the glory of God."

Is it time to sort out some of your busyness? Offer your schedule to the Father who loves you. Lay your to-do list on the altar as a gift of love to him. Sometimes he calls us to set aside our "fluttering behind us" to-do list. He created time. It never overwhelms him. It never stresses him. And he will give you all the time you need to accomplish the true purposes he has in mind for you. If you're overwhelmed to the freak-out point, it's not because he has put too many things on your list; it's because you have.

Pray It Through

Pray through your list, whether written or mental, and ask the Lord what should stay and what should go. Ask him to help you sort your necessary from the unnecessary, the truly worthwhile and praise-worthy from those things that are not. When we let the busyness of the not-so-worthwhile take over our schedules, we miss out on the truly worthwhile and the things worthy of praise. Ask him which items on your list are within his purpose for you and which aren't.

Pray even as you do the tasks on your list, asking the Father to receive glory in your work. Trudging through your overwhelming busyness without seeking him will leave you unequipped to accomplish anything of value in any way that pleases him and unprepared for any little surprise shreddings and extra demands along the way. Stay in constant touch with the Lord, leaning on him every step.

Isaiah 40:31 gives us a word of encouragement:

> But those who wait for the Lord [who expect, look for, and hope in Him] shall change and renew their strength and power; they shall

lift their wings and mount up [close to God] as eagles [mount up to the sun]; they shall run and not be weary, they shall walk and not faint or become tired.

AMP

From Overwhelmed to . . . Overwhelmed

When it makes you tired just to think about your schedule and you feel you're being pulled in a gajillion different directions, there's only one right direction—his. Wait on the Lord, look to him, hope in him, draw your strength and power from him—the power to do the things you really need to do, and the wisdom to know what to cross off the list. Drawing close to him is the cure for the fatigue of busyness. You don't need to bow to the hubbub. You need to bow before him. Bowing before his presence will bring a peace into your life that will overwhelm you. It's a completely different kind of "overwhelmed."

Psalm 90:12 is a great verse to put at the top of every to-do list: "Teach us to make the most of our time, so that we may grow in wisdom" (NLT[a]). We need his wisdom for his timing. And the more we adopt his timing, the more we have his wisdom.

Incidentally, any time the Lord encourages you to shred your list, let me know. LuLu delivers.

> Unless the LORD builds a house,
> the work of the builders is wasted.
> Unless the LORD protects a city,
> guarding it with sentries will do no good.
> It is useless for you to work so hard
> from early morning until late at night,
> anxiously working for food to eat;
> for God gives rest to his loved ones.

Psalm 127:1–2 NLT[b]

27 Keeps Me Blinging as I Go

Stress

The first time I saw a commercial on TV for a "Bedazzler," I confess I was totally bedazzled. I was completely lost in thoughts of blinging here, blinging there, blinging, blinging, everywhere. I could add jewels to my purses, shoes, scarves—we're talking about accessorizing the accessories! I was looking at a future bling-o-rama for sure. And it wouldn't have to stop with accessories. I pictured my very own bejeweled laptop, glittering tennis racket, a rhinestone-studded toaster. Why not bejewel the trash dumpster? The gutters, porch, and surrounding trees! So many bedazzling possibilities all through the neighborhood!

Before I picked up the phone to dial the Bedazzler 800 number, though, I had to rein in my dialing finger. Alas, it occurred to me (and I don't think this will surprise anyone) that I might get carried away. I could no doubt find myself in such an utter bling-glut that I could interfere with satellite signals all over my hemisphere. I can envision all cell phone reception blocked in my county. I imagined myself armed with a Bedazzler. In a holster. With rounds of jewels crisscrossing my body Rambo-style, ready to fling bling on an entire unsuspecting city that might not really want all that extra sparkle. *Put down the bling gun and slowly step away.*

That much over-blinging—would it be safe? It stressed me out a bit just to think about it. I finally sighed and decided not to order. Bling crisis averted.

Bang the Gavel

Every once in a while, I tend to shut down when I get stressed. If I were on trial for it, my houseplants could be Exhibit A.

"WORTHWHILE AND WORTHY OF PRAISE"

I'm the worst at getting distracted by life's hubbub and giving up on my plants. Didn't I see a movie one time about some sort of radioactive incident that brought a monstrous plant to cognizant life? Honestly, I hope that never happens to mine. If plants ever take over the world, I am so doomed. The plants would no doubt count me as the equivalent of a concentration camp guard.

Picture my trial, testimony after testimony from pitiful brownish-yellow, crunchy life-forms. For all the atrocities I've committed against plant-life-dom, I would no doubt spend the rest of my life in a cold, dark, plant-less prison, incarcerated for crimes against vegetation. Whoa, that's a stressful thought too.

Busyness vs. Stress

We looked at busyness in the last chapter, but let's take an extra look at stress. Busyness and stress are related, but not exactly the same. Busyness has to do with demands and trials and the frustrations that come with living a fast-paced life in a fast-paced culture. It's tiptoeing around an agenda that requires a lot from us.

While busyness can definitely be a stressor, stress is more about how we perceive and respond to our challenges and difficulties. And different challenges stress people in different ways and at different levels. We all respond to stress individually.

Two Different Stresses

Some stress does result from busyness and living in a culture that's busy to the max. That's the kind of stress that can actually often be a motivator. It can inspire us to achieve, to push ourselves further to succeed. We can even let those kinds of stressors work for us instead of against us.

Other stresses come from painful or out-of-control circumstances like a financial crisis or a difficult job situation, a family catastrophe or heartbreak, a serious illness—those kinds of life situations we have little or no power to change. Sometimes it's that out-of-control factor that stresses us the most.

How Should We Respond to Stress?

If we will allow it to happen, when we can respond with grace in the midst of those smaller stressors—breaking a nail, running out of milk, getting cut off in traffic—we're learning to respond more graciously when the bigger stressors come along.

When you're experiencing pressures—whether they're mild or intense—thinking through the stress can help in surviving and thriving. Here are just a few points to ponder.

Notice your stress factors. What is it that gets your goat? Take note of how you're responding to stress. Do you ever experience fatigue, headaches, stomach problems, nervousness, insomnia, lack of concentration, irritability, or do you lose control of your emotions in response to stress?

How you deal with stress can affect how you eat, sleep, and interact with others. God has wired our mental and emotional health very closely with the physical. Proverbs 12:25 says, "An anxious heart weighs a man down." Dealing with stress in destructive ways can actually lead to poor physical health as well. Do you overeat when you're overwhelmed? Are you ever tempted to deal with stress by using alcohol or drugs? Do you make unhealthy or dangerous choices as a result of feeling stressed, frustrated, or snowed under? Unhealthy responses to stress should be like a tap on the shoulder, getting your attention. Heed the tap.

Take a few practical de-stressing steps. If busyness is your stressor, say some no's where you can and set some priorities. There is a right time and a right place—a right way to order your days. Ecclesiastes 8:5–6 says, "For a wise heart knows the proper time and procedure. For there is a proper time and procedure for every delight" (NASB).

Think about what might be a stress reliever for you. A bubble bath? Praise music? Taking a walk? A good book? Treat yourself to a healthy stress buster.

Wrap all those things in the Word of God. You'll find your greatest peace as you look to the God of peace. Fill your mind with his perfect instruction in the life of peace. "Your laws are perfect and completely trustworthy. . . . Your promises have been thoroughly tested; that is why I love them so much. . . . As pressure and stress bear down on me, I find joy in your commands" (Psalm 119:138, 140, 143 NLT[b]). His Word is completely trustworthy, peace-tested again and again. His promises and instruction offer peace even during periods of big-time stress.

Understand that it's okay to get help. If you're having trouble dealing with stress and you see harmful responses to your stressors, don't hesitate to seek help from a professional. That may be the first step for you in the direction of dealing well with your stress. Ask your pastor or a trusted friend to recommend a godly counselor.

Additionally, talking it all out with a godly friend you trust can go a long way in relieving stress. Share your burden. Proverbs 11:14 says, "Where no wise guidance is, the people fall, but in the multitude of counselors there is safety" (AMP). Even if your friend doesn't offer counsel, it can be a significant de-stressor to simply get some of those stresses off your chest.

Always run to the Lord. He is our great Counselor. First Peter 5:7 says, "Cast all your anxiety on him because he cares for you." Do you truly believe that God can help you through your every problem? Do you believe he can give you the strength you need to deal with whatever comes your way?

When we're stressed over feeling out of control, it's good to remember that it's really okay to be out of control—as long as he is in control. And he is. There is nothing in your life that escapes his attention—or his care. You can trust him even when you can't see the big picture.

Keep your mind on the worthwhile and praiseworthy. Do you often let the negative thoughts from those stress factors crowd out good and positive thoughts so that all you can see are your problems? If we want to experience peace, we must think like God thinks. The focus part of our Philippians passage reminds us, "Don't ever stop thinking about what is truly worthwhile and worthy of praise." There is peace in keeping our minds on the worthwhile and the praiseworthy.

Isaiah 26:3–4 says, "You will keep in perfect peace him whose mind is steadfast, because he trusts in you. Trust in the LORD forever, for the LORD, the LORD, is the Rock eternal." He is the never-wavering Rock. And anytime you're experiencing stress of any kind, you can look to the Rock.

Bedazzling Peace

Have you ever seen someone respond with great grace when they're in the midst of huge stressors? Have you ever been that person who responds with grace? Have you seen the peace of God lavished on you or on a stressed friend until it shines in all directions? The Lord, our Rock, lavishes that peace. And his peace truly can shine like nothing bedazzled we've ever seen!

> I've picked you. I haven't dropped you. Don't panic. I'm with you. There's no need to fear for I'm your God. I'll give you strength. I'll help you. I'll hold you steady, keep a firm grip on you. . . . That's right. Because I, your God, have a firm grip on you and I'm not letting go. I'm telling you, "Don't panic. I'm right here to help you."
>
> Isaiah 41:9–10, 13 Message

28 VIRTUAL GEMS

Witnessing

Someone actually sent me some e-bling recently. Pictures of diamond, ruby, and emerald jewelry via email? Nice, but I'm afraid it's nothing

"WORTHWHILE AND WORTHY OF PRAISE"

like getting the real thing. You can't wear e-jewelry. Putting it on your virtual self is simply not the same. And even though the e-note said I would be a crummy friend if I didn't forward it on to a couple dozen of my closest friends and family, I kept the e-jewels to myself.

I might as well go ahead and confess: I am not a forwarder. I check my email faithfully—even read most of it. But despite threats of gazillions of missed blessings and surefire calamities if I don't "forward this to 10 people in the next 3 minutes," I still do not forward. And guess what. I'm still here. I haven't noticed any missed blessings (though in all fairness, how would I really notice them if I never got them?). No more calamities than usual either. I haven't even had any kidneys stolen as far as I know. Despite my forwarding rebellion, the bird of paradise has never flown up my nose—or whatever in the world they're saying will happen this week.

I've never bought into the empty e-promises of "luck" (give me a break), and I never once believed that Bill Gates would send me money. I've turned down thousands of dollars in "no obligation" gift cards, and I didn't even cave when I was promised I would lose ten pounds just by reading about a free weight-loss plan. And would you believe my spam filter is set ridiculously high?

My Spam Filter Is Set on Stun

I cranked up the filter when I woke up one morning to 3,000 email messages in one of my accounts. Not even good messages. All goofy. I had been spammed but good. Not just your basic spam, but one of those evil e-things that keeps on giving. I was over 5,000 by noon. I set my email filter up a notch. Still more goofy messages. Up another notch. They kept coming. When it was on the highest setting and they still kept coming, I have to admit I found myself looking around in the spam filter choices for a setting called STUN.

Sorting through all the e-silliness sometimes agitates the stuffing out of me. I've decided if I'm going to forward—to pass something on—it's going to have to be something believable. And not just believable, but worthwhile. As a matter of fact, unless I find something eternally worthwhile, I just can't bring myself to press that Send button.

Being "sent" doesn't cause agitation if Jesus is the one doing the sending. In John 20:21, the resurrected Jesus said, "Peace be with you! As the Father has sent me, I am sending you."

A Sending That's So Very Worthwhile

His peace is the opposite of agitation. And what a privilege to be sent on such a worthy peace mission by the Savior himself. His sending gives us the mission of passing on, sending forward, his message of salvation. Eternally worthwhile!

Have you ever had the thrill of delivering a message that you found stunning? Not the "set your spam filter on stun" kind of stunning, but a truly jaw-dropping truth that has the power to change lives? The message of God's love and peace really is stunning. Who would expect a holy God to show such startling mercy? Ephesians 2:4–5 says, "Because of his great love for us, God, who is rich in mercy, made us alive with Christ." I love the way the Message phrases it: "Immense in mercy and with an incredible love, he embraced us."

It's the mind-boggling caress of God! He embraced us by his love and mercy. And this loving, merciful hug of God gently wraps us and holds us tenderly in his peace.

Forward It On

How can we not share it? Thinking about what is truly worthwhile and worthy of praise includes remembering Jesus's suffering and his humiliating death on the cross. The sinless Christ hung on a cross, hated and shamed, bearing our sin so we could have peace with a holy God.

Then God came up with the plan to get the word out about the salvation that's available through that sacrificial death. He could've sent it exclusively through email. He could've designed a plan to have scrolls unfurl from heaven. He could've written it in the stars or broadcast it over every satellite. But he commissioned the job to us. He honored us by allowing us to participate in the sharing plan. And in the light of all he's done to provide our salvation, is it too much to ask that we share it? And considering what's at stake for those with whom we share, is it too much to ask?

Is That Real?

If our faith in Christ is genuine and if his salvation is the real deal, then it's not too much to ask that we share the good news with others. It's just not.

Our faith is the truest gem. No e-fakery. Our salvation is based on the truth of God's Word, and when we genuinely come to faith in him, our lives are never the same. Life ceases to be about the temporary and takes on new meaning and passion—all wrapped in his amazing peace. What a message!

It's a radical life change that's worth forwarding. It's an honor and a blessing to tell others what Christ has done for us and to model the changes he's made by living a Christ-filled, God-rearranged life before them. What can better testify that Jesus changes lives than a living illustration of a life that has been changed?

Virtual Blessing

How did you come to faith in Christ? Was it modeled before you? Have you seen it modeled before you since you became a believer? Have you ever seen God work in someone's life through the testimony of what he's done in your life? There's virtually no greater blessing.

All e-messages aside, we all share a calling to forward the message. We're chosen to tell. First Peter 2:9 says, "You were chosen to tell about the wonderful acts of God, who called you out of darkness into his wonderful light" (NCV). As those who've been called out of darkness and into his light, we've been given the real thing. We get to help turn on the lights for those in darkness. And Isaiah 52:7 tells us it's beautiful when we share that peace-giving good news: "How beautiful on the mountains are the feet of those who bring good news, who proclaim peace, who bring good tidings, who proclaim salvation, who say to Zion, 'Your God reigns!'"

With email, with trumpets, with satellites—let's use it all to share the worthwhile, praiseworthy message of salvation with everyone who will listen. Let's use our words. Psalm 89:1–2 says, "I will sing of the LORD's great love forever; with my mouth I will make your faithfulness known through all generations. I will declare that your love stands firm forever, that you established your faithfulness in heaven itself."

Hey, now *that's* worth forwarding!

> Hallelujah! Thank GOD! Pray to him by name!
>   Tell everyone you meet what he has done!
> Sing him songs, belt out hymns,
>   translate his wonders into music!
> Honor his holy name with Hallelujahs,
>   you who seek GOD. Live a happy life!
> Keep your eyes open for GOD, watch for his works;
>   be alert for signs of his presence.
> Remember the world of wonders he has made,
>   his miracles, and the verdicts he's rendered—
>   O seed of Abraham, his servant,
>   O child of Jacob, his chosen.
>
> Psalm 105:1–6 Message

Loving Things

It's a good thing I'm not a bling snob. I lose too many pieces of my not-so-fine jewelry to invest in a lot of the good stuff. I've deposited necklaces, rings, pins, and earrings from one side of this country to the other. I'm practically leaving a trail.

Thankfully, every time I come up a piece or two short, costume jewelry is easy enough to replace. For every minor bling emergency, there's always a Wal-Mart. Always.

It's nice too that they stock more than just emergency bling. Tires, windshield wipers, and emergency vanity mirrors. Drinks, snacks, and emergency chocolate. Batteries, power cords, and emergency iPods. When we travel as a family, we map our trail from emergency Wal-Mart stop to emergency Wal-Mart stop.

Wally-cation

We got home just last week from this summer's family vacation. We drove—would you believe it—1,100 miles in one day. I know there are those of you Wonder Women who've done more. I am not worthy. I'm not one of those "get there with no stops" kinds of travelers. One thousand one hundred miles. Do you know how many Wal-Mart stops that is? Or an even bigger question, do you know how many gas station restroom stops that is? And do you know how disgusting a gas station restroom can be? There's not enough hand sanitizer in all the Wal-Marts in all the land to fix that. By the first 500 miles I was encouraging all my kids to "think dry thoughts."

"Just 600 more miles, guys, you can hold it." I got home feeling like I needed a vacation. And a *drum* of hand sanitizer.

Think Dry

Okay, so "thinking dry thoughts" might not be all that effective. But it's another reminder that we do need to pay close attention to what we think. Our thoughts matter. It's all too easy to miss the worthwhile and praiseworthy thoughts and get distracted by sparkly things instead. It's not our jewelry or our looks that inspire worthwhile thinking. First Peter 3:3–4 says,

> Your beauty should not come from outward adornment, such as braided hair and the wearing of gold jewelry and fine clothes. Instead, it should be that of your inner self, the unfading beauty of a gentle and quiet spirit, which is of great worth in God's sight.

Becoming beautiful to the heavenly Father—now that's worthwhile. It's what's on the inside that counts. A gentle and quiet spirit is a spirit at peace. It boomerangs right back around to peace, doesn't it! We can never allow our peace to be wrapped up in what we have—things and blings will come and go. When we learn to hang on to the eternal, that's when we become wealthy in spirit and satisfied right down to the soul.

Ecclesiastes 5:10 says, "Whoever loves money never has money enough; whoever loves wealth is never satisfied with his income." Caught up in money and things? You'll find yourself never satisfied, never at peace. Peace comes with the understanding of exactly where our true riches lie, those things that are truly worthwhile and worthy of praise. Luke 12:15 says, "Life is not defined by what you have, even when you have a lot" (Message).

Now There's Value

The moment we surrendered our hearts to Jesus, our lives took on new value. We were purchased with the life of the Son of God himself. Knowing him gives us a wealth not limited to this side of our heartbeat. Philippians 3:8 says, "All things are worth nothing compared with the greatness of knowing Christ Jesus my Lord" (NCV).

Becoming focused on getting more and more stuff will leave us less and less satisfied. The first part of that passage in Luke 12:15 warns to "be on your guard against every form of greed" (NASB). It always takes just a little more to keep up with the Joneses.

Can we find satisfaction in just the right bling? Nope—not even in a mountain of it. As we follow the Lord, our Shepherd, we find everything we need. And when our focus is clearly on following him, we also find that we have everything we really want. "The LORD is my shepherd; I shall not want" (Ps. 23:1 NKJV). Resting in the care of the Shepherd results in satisfaction, contentment—a life at peace.

From Store to Re-stored

Looking to things—even looking to other people—for fulfillment or validation will still leave us wanting. Possessions can't meet our eternal needs. Not all the goods on all the shelves at the super-est Wal-Mart can give us everything we need. Neither can people. It's only in the Shepherd we experience a soul restored (Ps. 23:3). We need to keep our eyes focused and our thoughts in tune with the truly worthwhile. Psalm 119:37 says, "Turn my eyes away from worthless things; preserve my life according to your word."

How many women are heartsick over their lack of personal peace but have yet to put their finger on the reason they lack it? They haven't come to grips with their love of the temporary. And how many have realized their love for the temporary but still haven't let go of the temporary to embrace the eternal peace that the Shepherd offers?

We'll never find peace in the riches the world has to offer. Proverbs 13:7 says, "There is one who makes himself rich, yet has nothing; And one who makes himself poor, yet has great riches"

(NKJV). Oswald Chambers addressed it so well in *My Utmost for His Highest*:

> Are you seeking great things for yourself, instead of seeking to be a great person? God wants you to be in a much closer relationship with Himself than simply receiving His gifts—He wants you to get to know Him. Even some large thing we want is only incidental; it comes and it goes. But God never gives us anything incidental. There is nothing easier than getting into the right relationship with God, unless it is not God you seek, but only what He can give you.[1]

Store Managers?

Since God is the creator of everything, he owns it all. What is really completely ours? He loves to bless us with good things, but we're more managers than we are owners, and even our managing should be done according to his desires. His priorities should show up in the checkbook register, in the jewelry box, and on every shopping list. Does saying no to things ever seem unreasonable to you? To meet our needs for food and shelter, we need to earn money and use that money. God has instructed us to do that, and we're not being obedient when we don't work to meet the needs of our family. But we live in a culture that says that's not enough. We're not satisfied with provision. We want more and bigger and better.

It's not sinful to have things. The Lord loves to bless. It doesn't become sin until we *love* those things. First Timothy 6:10 spells it out: "For the love of money is a root of all kinds of evil." It all starts in the mind. A self-centered philosophy of earning and having and spending will lead to all kinds of evil. A Christ-centered philosophy will open up doors of generosity and blessing. We need to remember that when we have him, we have everything we need. Hebrews 13:5 is a great reminder: "Keep your lives free from the love of money and be content with what you have, because God has said, 'Never will I leave you; never will I forsake you.'"

"WORTHWHILE AND WORTHY OF PRAISE"

No matter how many miles we may travel in this life (and whether all those miles are in one day or not), the Lord is with us, ready to satisfy with great peace. Lining up our thinking and our priorities with his will brings great contentment.

Lots of bling, little bling, bling scattered across the country. It just doesn't matter. Paul said in Philippians 4:11, "I have learned in whatever state I am, to be content" (NKJV).

By the way, driving 1,100 miles in one day will mean that you have several states in which to be content. Always.

> Yet true godliness with contentment is itself great wealth. After all, we brought nothing with us when we came into the world, and we can't take anything with us when we leave it. So if we have enough food and clothing, let us be content.
>
> But people who long to be rich fall into temptation and are trapped by many foolish and harmful desires that plunge them into ruin and destruction. For the love of money is the root of all kinds of evil. And some people, craving money, have wandered from the true faith and pierced themselves with many sorrows.
>
> 1 Timothy 6:6–12 NLT[b]

Engineering 30 the Earrings

Laziness vs. the Peace of Purpose

I caught one of my daughters in a rebellious act of accessorization recently. She was wearing earrings that . . . and this is difficult to say

... earrings that ... didn't match. Where did I go wrong? It was bad enough that they didn't match her outfit, but the really bad part was that they didn't even match *each other*.

Surely she knew not what she had done. I said, "Allie, you're going to die when I tell you this, but did you know that you're wearing two different earrings?"

"Oh yeah, I know. I couldn't find the mate to my favorite pair so I just popped in this one."

"You couldn't find the mate to the second one either?"

"Yeah, it was in there."

"Well, Allie, why didn't you wear that one, then—even though they don't go with what you're wearing (hint, hint)—at least you'd have a matching pair."

"Eh. They're fine."

Fine? *Fine?* And I had tried so hard to be a good mother.

It's not rocket science. Earrings are supposed to match. Wasn't it the height of accessory laziness? And she had the nerve to laugh when I started talking about scheduling an intervention.

I've Got Their Numbers

Allie's not the only one. Soon after the mismatched earrings incident, my son Daniel needed to make a call and I told him to look up the number in the phone book. He just stared at me, blinking a couple of times for accent. Then he half-whined, "Can't we get the number from the Internet?"

I handed him the phone book and watched as he rolled his eyes. He sighed, then started simultaneously thumbing through the pages and reciting his alphabet. It was like he hadn't done it in years. And you would've thought I'd asked him to write a phone-book-length research paper.

Is it just me, or does there seem to be a laziness epidemic? I wonder if it's being exacerbated by texting and email. We can't even find the motivation to use capital letters anymore. When we do press the cap key, we lock it in and they're *all* caps—which means, of course, that we're text-yelling. In addition to misused caps, entire words have been reported missing from the English language. "You" and "are" are now "u" and "r," just to cite a couple.

Chillin' with the La-Z-Boys

Did the turn toward laziness hit our culture with the invention of the television? After all, I don't remember anyone ever needing a foil-covered dinner shortcut before TV. No one ever thought it necessary to invent "radio dinners."

Whenever it happened, laziness appears to be the norm these days. Our culture's motto is "just chill." Accomplishing great things is much less popular. I guess that's why you'll likely never see an "Ambitious-Boy" recliner.

Wondering if you might be waddling toward the lazy side? Put off that gazillionth game of computer solitaire, read through the top ten laziness indicators, and give yourself a little test. Incidentally, if you can't make yourself read through all ten, that could be the first clue.

Top Ten Signs You Might Be Lazy

1. Your favorite book has always been *How to Do Nothing and Still Make Millions*.
2. You hired a personal assistant to read the book *How to Do Nothing and Still Make Millions* for you.
3. You spend long hours observing your cat and learning his ways.
4. You watch TV as many hours as you sleep . . . and some think instead of sleeping, you're actually hibernating.
5. Your house catches fire and the three things you tell your personal assistant to run in and save for you are the microwave, the remote control, and your pillow-top mattress.

6. Someone tells you there's a great sunset out the west window and you're disappointed . . . since you're looking east.
7. You dread having to get up early for that afternoon appointment.
8. You can't find the remote, so you end up watching 18 straight hours of *Petticoat Junction*.
9. You finally decide to give up on the *Make Millions* book and have your personal assistant pick up a copy of *The Slacker's Manual* instead.
10. You tell people you're actually doing a scientific experiment involving inertia.

Maybe it is all about inertia and the science of it all. I saw a T-shirt that said, "I might look like I'm doing nothing, but at the cellular level I'm actually quite busy."

Instead of cell-watching or cat-watching, God's Word tells us to do some ant-watching—to learn from the ant, not the cat.

> You lazy people can learn by watching an anthill. Ants don't have leaders, but they store up food during harvest season. How long will you lie there doing nothing at all? When are you going to get up and stop sleeping?
>
> Proverbs 6:6–9 CEV

The lazy person's mantra in that passage, incidentally, is "Sleep a little. Doze a little. Fold your hands and twiddle your thumbs" (v. 10 CEV). It's like the couch potato's rap.

Couch Potatoes Are Vegetables

Work is God-ordained. Resistance to it came with the fall and the curse of sin, but even before the fall, God gave Adam jobs to do. They were fulfilling. I imagine naming the animals would've been entertaining work. Genesis 2:15 tells us, "The LORD God took the man and put him in the Garden of Eden to work it and take care of it," so Adam was working the ground, growing potatoes even before the invention of the couch.

A society full of people who won't work will never succeed. We need hard workers in the world to make it work. Our heavenly Father expects us to work. And he expects us to honor him in that work. Should it surprise us that peace is found in doing a good job, not in wasting energy avoiding it? Ecclesiastes 2:24 says, "A man can do nothing better than to eat and drink and find satisfaction in his work. This too, I see, is from the hand of God."

We're certainly not called to be workaholics. But God does call us to work. He has a purpose for you in your work. Ephesians 2:10 says, "God has made us what we are. In Christ Jesus, God made us to do good works, which God planned in advance for us to live our lives doing" (NCV).

Work the Plan

When you discover his plan for you, you discover his peace right there with it, along with satisfaction and joy. Galatians 6:4 says, "But let every person carefully scrutinize and examine and test his own conduct and his own work. He can then have the personal satisfaction and joy of doing something commendable" (AMP).

Rest is important and we all need to know when to take a break. But laziness is resting more than we were ever meant to rest and in exactly the wrong way. Some think that kicking back and doing nothing for as long as we want sounds peaceful, but slothfulness brings the exact opposite of peace. It brings frustration in all our missed accomplishments, guilt over not doing what we know we should've done, sadness over the fruitlessness of not fulfilling our calling in Christ.

Where should our rest be? Peace only comes from resting in Christ and in passionately pursuing his calling on our lives. Sometimes we're busy right through the rest, but we're never at a loss for peace. There's perfect peace in being exactly where we were meant to be. By resting in Christ, we actually build muscle—and that will keep laziness at a safe distance. "Strengthen yourselves so that you will live here on earth doing what God wants" (1 Peter 4:2 NCV).

Find satisfaction in the job the Father has given you. Find peace in fulfilling your purpose. Find joy in pleasing him.

And also: find the oomph to match up your earrings before your mom sees you. It might help you avoid an intervention.

> Go to the ant, you sluggard;
>> consider its ways and be wise!
> It has no commander,
>> no overseer or ruler,
> yet it stores its provisions in summer
>> and gathers its food at harvest.
> How long will you lie there, you sluggard?
>> When will you get up from your sleep?
> A little sleep, a little slumber,
>> a little folding of the hands to rest—
> and poverty will come on you like a bandit
>> and scarcity like an armed man.
>
> Proverbs 6:6–11

PART 7

"YOU KNOW THE TEACHINGS
I GAVE YOU, AND YOU KNOW
WHAT YOU HEARD ME SAY
AND SAW ME DO. SO FOLLOW
MY EXAMPLE."

Friend or Faux? 31

Following the Example,
Becoming the Example

They're common jewelry questions:

Is that imitation or is it real?
24-karat gold or 2-karat gold paint?
Diamond or diamond-esque?
Silver or lead?
Will it cut glass or *is* it cut glass?
Natural or cultured?
Sterling or stainless?
Paper or plastic?

How Should I "Brooch" the Subject?

I have friends who can tell the real from the faux. Personally I can't tell a fine piece of amber from a hunk of wood with a nice varnish. But if my jewel-savvy friends noticed me sporting a "fine" pin made of driftwood, do you suppose they would tell me it's not real? And how exactly would they "brooch" the subject?

I do have an oh-so-faux pin that I'll admit is a little on the loud side, but I like it anyway. Real rubies? Hardly. As a matter of fact, if you look at it from far away, it looks more like I took a reflector off one of the kids' bicycles and pinned it on my coat. At least I'm less likely to get hit by a car. Sometimes faux works.

Even though I'm not so in-the-know about faux, I see it everywhere. Imitation jewels, imitation furs, imitation leather—we have imitation crab, imitation cheese, and imitation vanilla flavor. And can we even count the number of offers we see every day for "genuine imitation designer knockoff dead-ringer" products from every category, group, classification, and genus rank on every molecular level?

Imitation of a Different Species

Paul encourages us in a different kind of imitation. His tone in his instruction takes a bit of a different tack in Philippians 4:9. He says, "You know the teachings I gave you, and you know what you heard me say and saw me do. So follow my example" (CEV). Paul lays down the specifics in how we should think and then moves to the effect of that thinking and the example.

It's one thing to hear the principles taught and another to see them lived out. In essence, what Paul taught and what people heard him say and saw him do were all in sync. Nothing fake with Paul. He was the genuine article. Actually, his was a "genuine imitation"—of Christ. So genuine that he could say to the believers he loved, "Look at the way I live and do what I'm doing—look, listen, learn, and do."

We're living according to our calling in Christ when we follow Paul's example because Paul followed Jesus's example. And then God's glorious plan kicks in before we even know it—and we *become* the example for others to follow. Imitation in the round!

Genuine Imitation

Do you suppose the people who hold to the adage that imitation is the sincerest form of flattery have ever heard karaoke? That's imitation on an entirely different note. The imitation Paul is encouraging is not only the sincerest form of flattery but the sincerest form of obedience. Follow Jesus. Then know the blessing of seeing others follow you.

That's how it happened in Thessalonica. Paul commends them in 1 Thessalonians 1:6–8:

> You became imitators of us and of the Lord; in spite of severe suffering, you welcomed the message with the joy given by the Holy Spirit. And so you became a model to all the believers in Macedonia and Achaia. The Lord's message rang out from you not only in Macedonia and Achaia—your faith in God has become known everywhere.

They imitated Paul and the other teachers, imitated the Lord, and then, neglecting hardships, became the examples for others to follow.

Everyone Follows

There are two directions we can go as believers. We can follow Jesus, focus on walking in obedience and growing in our relationship with him, or we can follow the direction of friends or media or the culture in general and compromise our convictions. Follow Jesus or follow selfishness and the world—not following is not a choice.

The further into worldly influences a person travels, the more "right" those worldly ways seem. One ignored biblical principle leads to a blatant disregard of another, and sooner or later, sin has a grip. The attention once focused on the Lord is won away by the distractions of self-centered living. A believer who is indulging in self-centered living instead of following Christ in God-centered living has been rendered useless in the kingdom of God. A person indulging in sin and selfishness will eventually destroy her reputation. Nothing worth following there.

Could I encourage you not to yield to that "self," worldly way of thinking? The second you give in to it, you forfeit your peace. Follow the true Leader instead. Imitate the Father, the only one who is holy and the only one who loves you with a perfect love. Ephesians 5:1 says, "Be imitators of God, therefore, as dearly loved children."

Follow the Leader—with All Your Heart

David experienced times of peace-less disobedience and times of blessed following. He prayed in Psalm 86:11, "Teach me your way, O Lord, and I will walk in your truth; give me an undivided heart, that I may fear your name."

When we read "heart" in the Bible, we're not reading about cardiac muscle. When David asked the Lord for an undivided heart in this psalm, he wasn't asking for a healthy and whole cardiovascular system. No, he was asking God for thoughts, desires, goals, beliefs, and every direction of his life—every part of his being—to be wholly focused on godliness. He was asking to think like God thinks. He was asking the Father to teach him what he needed to know so that he could imitate his holy God.

Are you ready to ask the Lord for an undivided heart? Take a look at your life. Do the things you say and do line up with your beliefs? Ask him to realign your thoughts, desires, goals, beliefs, direction, and to keep it all wholly focused on him. Ask him to line up your thinking with his thinking. Ask him to give you everything you need to look, listen, learn, and do.

It's my heart's desire that my life will consistently reflect love for and obedience to Christ. And what a blessing it would be to see others drawn to imitate that.

Oh, and with its imitation of a reflector, that faux pin on my coat is doing a great job of warding off cars for me.

> Watch what God does, and then you do it, like children who learn proper behavior from their parents. Mostly what God does is love you. Keep company with him and learn a life of love. Observe how Christ loved us. His love was not cautious but extravagant. He didn't love in order to get something from us but to give everything of himself to us. Love like that.

"FOLLOW MY EXAMPLE"

Don't allow love to turn into lust, setting off a downhill slide into sexual promiscuity, filthy practices, or bullying greed. Though some tongues just love the taste of gossip, those who follow Jesus have better uses for language than that. Don't talk dirty or silly. That kind of talk doesn't fit our style. Thanksgiving is our dialect.

You can be sure that using people or religion or things just for what you can get out of them—the usual variations on idolatry—will get you nowhere, and certainly nowhere near the kingdom of Christ, the kingdom of God.

Don't let yourselves get taken in by religious smooth talk. God gets furious with people who are full of religious sales talk but want nothing to do with him. Don't even hang around people like that.

You groped your way through that murk once, but no longer. You're out in the open now. The bright light of Christ makes your way plain. So no more stumbling around. Get on with it! The good, the right, the true—these are the actions appropriate for daylight hours. Figure out what will please Christ, and then do it.

Ephesians 5:1–10 Message

Improper 32
Gem Shopper

*Paul's Example of Strength
through Weakness*

Have you ever had your head nearly taken off by a rogue jewelry shopper? A clearance jewelry table at a nice department store can be a brawl just waiting to happen. A two-fer? It could get ugly. Buy a necklace, get free earrings? Katy bar the door! Someone could lose an earlobe. Totally improper.

The improper shoppers are not exclusively at jewelry clearance tables in nice department stores either. Customers everywhere these days can be merciless. Savvy consumers? They're too often more like savage consumers. The other day I'd been wrestling my two-ton shopping cart for way too long at the super center. I was looking for a checkout lane with less than a *multitude* of people in it, biblically speaking. I was hoping to get out of the store sometime before the next dawn.

Then suddenly, oh glory of glories, the checker in the "20 items or less" lane had a miraculous break in her line. She motioned me and my semi-truck-sized cart over to her lane. I felt like the Red Sea had just parted. It was a spiritual moment.

No sooner had I unloaded one of the two tons, when a long line of those genuine "20 items or less" shoppers slipped in behind me. Angrily. I could feel them counting. I wanted to say, "Look, guys, she motioned me over," but I decided against it. Why drag the checker down with me? I decided against eye contact all together. After all, I was in a store that sold hunting artillery. I opted for staying quiet and trying not to hyperventilate. As soon as my purchases were paid for and reloaded, I shot to the car, maneuvering my two-ton cart at breakneck speed . . . in a serpentine manner. Everyone knows a swerving target is tougher to hit.

Stranger Danger

Road rage? Puh! *Lane rage*—now there's some danger. I would've been reasonably okay with a "shop 'til you drop" kind of day. I've had those before. But this was potentially a "shop 'til someone drops you" scenario. Somehow that was so much scarier.

Embarrassing as it is to admit, sometimes I'm the improper shopper. More on the "stranger" side than the "danger" side. I guess we're all tempted every now and then to slough off the hero role and take the low road. The Lone Ranger gets shoved aside for the Lane Rager. The temptation to whine and complain, rant, rave, and rage suddenly appears. Hello, out-of-control emotions.

"Follow my Example"

Paul challenges us to follow his example. What kind of emotional control did he model? It was Paul who, inspired by the Holy Spirit, wrote the words in Philippians 2:14, "Do everything without complaining or arguing."

In Control When Life Is Not

Paul is also one who experienced mind-boggling hardships and all kinds of cruelty at the hands of others. He lists some of those hardships in 2 Corinthians 11:23–27. He had done time in too many prisons, been beaten more times than he could count, thought time after time that his number was up and he was about to die. He had been given the traditional thirty-nine stripes by the Jews five times, taken to the point of death again and again. Three times he was beaten with rods, and he'd even been stoned and left for dead. I can't imagine surviving a shipwreck, yet Paul did it three times, once left floating in the sea, not for three or four hours, not even nine or ten, but for twenty-four hours.

He faced constant danger from natural disasters, thieves and thugs, religious zealots and pagans alike—even so-called believers who betrayed him. In the streets, in the deserts, on the seas—danger, danger, danger. He experienced exhaustion, pain, hunger and thirst, cold and lack of clothing.

If anyone had a case for legitimate complaining, no one would argue that Paul did. But that's not how he responded. He responded admirably. Properly. How did he do it? How did he keep control when life was out of control? And how can we?

What do you do when you're tempted to complain, criticize, or lash out in anger? Acknowledge the emotions, sure. But acknowledging them isn't enough. We've already looked at how our roller-coaster negative emotions will take over if we let them. We need to be ready to go a step further and respond well to the nasty negative emotions of others too.

Who's in Control?

To be women of integrity instead of women ruled by emotions, we need to identify who's really in control—and we need to make sure it's not us. Recognizing our own weakness, and surrendering every response, every emotion, to the control of the Holy Spirit will empower us to choose responses of grace and great faith.

Look at the response when Paul asked to be healed of his "thorn in the flesh" in 2 Corinthians 12:9–10:

> But he [the Lord] said to me, "My grace is sufficient for you, for my power is made perfect in weakness." Therefore I will boast all the more gladly about my weaknesses, so that Christ's power may rest on me. That is why, for Christ's sake, I delight in weaknesses, in insults, in hardships, in persecutions, in difficulties. For when I am weak, then I am strong.

Paul modeled great strength. But he modeled strength in weakness. To recognize our human weakness and to depend on divine strength is to possess true, life-altering power. And that example of Paul's strength in weakness is the example we need to follow. When we recognize our weakness, Christ is strong in us.

Growing Spiritual Muscle through Weakness

Can you praise God in your illness with as much passion and fervor as you can from a healthy body? Can you sing to him from a dark, cold prison the same as you can from the comfort of your nice, warm home? Can you worship him from your cross? How much do you love him? How completely do you depend on him? If you allow it, he will be your strength!

We can be in control when life is out of control as we surrender in worship to him and as we find our joy only in him. Emotional imbalance happens when we operate in our own strength, doing our own thing instead of operating in the power of the Spirit. When we yield everything that we have and everything that we are—weak though it all is—through his divine muscle, he gives us absolutely everything we need to accomplish all that we need to do.

No doubt he can strengthen us for any task beyond what we need.

Even shopping. If we will trust in God's divine strength, we should see more shoppers of the happy variety and fewer running away in a serpentine manner.

> Satan's angel did his best to get me down; what he in fact did was push me to my knees. No danger then of walking around high and mighty! At first I didn't think of it as a gift, and begged God to remove it. Three times I did that, and then he told me,
> My grace is enough; it's all you need.
> My strength comes into its own in your weakness.
> Once I heard that, I was glad to let it happen. I quit focusing on the handicap and began appreciating the gift. It was a case of Christ's strength moving in on my weakness. Now I take limitations in stride, and with good cheer, these limitations that cut me down to size—abuse, accidents, opposition, bad breaks. I just let Christ take over! And so the weaker I get, the stronger I become.
>
> 2 Corinthians 12:7–10 Message

ACCESSING 33 THE ACCESSORIES

Forgetting the Old and Following the New

I frequently annoy myself by discovering the perfect accessories for a special event *after* I'm home from the event. And I find it all right inside my own jewelry box—just a day late. How can I so easily forget what I have?

If only we had computerized bling systems. How much easier would it be to match up the right bling with the right apparel if I just had the right program? Type in the outfit and press Enter, then *voilà!*—the computer could spit out the perfect accessory combo. Randomly choosing accessories would never do. But designating a little Random Access Memory? That could work!

Computerized Accessories?

I admit I currently have computers on the brain. It's because I recently bought a new one. I'm still learning to navigate my way around it. It's new and faster and (now this is really the best part) it's so much shinier and prettier than my old one. I can't give you a good reason for it—because there's not one—but having a pretty computer is important to me.

To intelligent, work-minded people, the term "computer accessories" typically means software—accessories have to do with "function" stuff. Personally, my kind of computer accessories are more often fluffy pink computer covers and glittery stick-ons—accessories are all about "fashion" stuff. For instance, I'm tickled pink that my new computer matches my favorite shoes. This computer is no random accessory.

Randomly Accessing the Memory

I'm afraid it's not all glitter and fun with the new computer, though. My RAM is not working all that well. Not the computer's RAM, my own personal RAM. Seems my memory access is much too random. I keep forgetting that some things are just different on this new machine.

Clicking one spot meant one thing on the old model, but it's something else altogether on the new one. Some of the processes on this computer just don't compute. I would be much more frustrated if it didn't match my shoes, so I'm trying to non-randomly remember that.

When Paul said to the Philippians, "You know the teachings I gave you, and you know what you heard me say and saw me do. So follow my example," many of those Philippians had to do some random access forgetting. They needed to forget the old life and the old ways they once followed. And to live the new way of life, they needed to access the right thought patterns. We need to access those patterns of thinking, too, and when we do, we're following the example Paul gave of living for Jesus.

Goodbye, Obsolete Old Way

In 2 Corinthians 7:1, Paul said, "Since we have these promises, dear friends, let us purify ourselves from everything that contaminates body and spirit, perfecting holiness out of reverence for God." The old way of unholy thinking and living? Deleted! Second Corinthians 5:17 says, "Therefore, if anyone is in Christ, he is a new creation; the old has gone, the new has come!"

We can live a new life as a new creation because of what Christ has done in our lives. Ephesians 2:18 says, "For through him [Jesus] we both have access to the Father by one Spirit."

Wow, total access to the source of all life!

Reprogramming, Anyone?

We need to constantly utilize that access to continue to program our thoughts in the Jesus way of thinking. As a "random access reminder," in the original language the word "follow" in Philippians 4:9 is in the present active imperative. That means this is not a onetime deal. We don't follow at the beginning, then later choose a different program. We're instructed to keep on following. And we're to keep on following no matter what the circumstances. We've seen Paul's long list of hardships. And it's good for us to remember that he wrote this book not from a cushy computer café but from the obscurity of a prison. Even from prison, Paul continued to follow.

Do you trust the Lord enough to follow with abandon? Do you believe with all your heart that he has a purpose for you? He tells us in Jeremiah 29:11, " 'For I know the plans I have for you,' says the LORD. 'They are plans for good and not for disaster, to give you a future and a hope' " (NLT[b]).

Do you believe that God has a good plan for you, even when life throws a curveball or two? His promise in Jeremiah 29:11 is a good plan. A purpose. Follow him, trust his plan. Paul would tell you that even from prison, it's a good plan. Philippians, one of his prison epistles, is a book filled with joy. There is joy and peace as we trust the God who pulls every random program together to make life work in the most glorious, fruit-filled, purposeful way.

Peace and Purpose in the Same Program

Second Thessalonians 1:11 says, "With this in mind, we constantly pray for you, that our God may count you worthy of his calling, and that by his power he may fulfill every good purpose of yours and every act prompted by your faith." Every good purpose is fulfilled by *his* power.

> O Lord, keep us praying with this in mind. May we be counted worthy of your gracious calling, filled with your power, by faith, fulfilling your purposes and plans for us.

Want peace and satisfaction in life? Don't follow that old random path. Consistently keep on following in the Jesus way, never forgetting what you have in Christ.

Remembering your accessories is not nearly as important. But I will say that I'm heading out for a day of shopping. I have to find a

"FOLLOW MY EXAMPLE"

cute laptop case that can accentuate the pink sparkles on my computer and still coordinate with my favorite shoes.

All this trouble is a clear sign that God has decided to make you fit for the kingdom. You're suffering now, but justice is on the way. When the Master Jesus appears out of heaven in a blaze of fire with his strong angels, he'll even up the score by settling accounts with those who gave you such a bad time. His coming will be the break we've been waiting for. Those who refuse to know God and refuse to obey the Message will pay for what they've done. Eternal exile from the presence of the Master and his splendid power is their sentence. But on that very same day when he comes, he will be exalted by his followers and celebrated by all who believe—and all because you believed what we told you. Because we know that this extraordinary day is just ahead, we pray for you all the time—pray that our God will make you fit for what he's called you to be, pray that he'll fill your good ideas and acts of faith with his own energy so that it all amounts to something. If your life honors the name of Jesus, he will honor you. Grace is behind and through all of this, our God giving himself freely, the Master, Jesus Christ, giving himself freely.

2 Thessalonians 1:5–12 Message

Apparel Peril 34

Difficulties

We jewelry wearers are risk takers. We live on the edge. It's a life of excitement and adventure. But life on the edge can have its own fear factor. For the sake of full disclosure, I should tell you flat out that wearing jewelry is not without its own brand of danger. Bling: it's not for the fainthearted.

As a matter of fact, some pieces should no doubt come with warning labels. If they did, these could be the terrible top ten.

Top Ten Jewelry Danger Warnings

1. Warning: May not be gravity friendly.
2. Do not freeze—but if you do, do not lick.
3. Caution: Remove before swimming as accessory may be compared to "cement shoes."
4. Warning: Strong wind gust may give flight dynamic to earrings causing accidental liftoff.
5. Do not wear near fire or flame as jewelry may become your new tattoo.
6. Caution: Do not wear near microwave oven—jewelry may reduce electromagnetic short waves and cook the wrong goose.
7. Do not wear on unstable foundation as geometric shifts have been noted.
8. Warning: Do not wear while on commercial flight as pilot. instrumentation may be affected—stray Des Moines flights have been located in Qatar.
9. Do not wear between strong magnetic poles—may cause planet to leave orbit.
10. Caution: Check atmospheric conditions before wearing—do not wear during electrical storm as you may be one lightning strike away from a total bling meltdown.

Though I've learned to walk on the danger side of the sparkles, I still get a little nervous when a thunderstorm rolls in. Do you know how much metal I'm wearing? I'm my own lightning rod. One stray bolt and almost any of my necklaces could permanently sear itself onto my chest.

Mega-jeweled women should probably avoid gathering in large groups altogether if lightning is present. Someone could end up with chicken-fried bangs, for sure.

Hair on a Different Front

Bangs are risky business even without the added volts. You wouldn't believe how much I have to go through to get just the right hair look. Gelling, teasing, moussing, ironing, spraying—folding, spindling, and mutilating—everything just short of taking the entire coif to the kiln at the ceramic shop for a good firing.

How frustrating to finally get the exact hair look I'm going for, only to take the hand mirror and back up to the bathroom mirror to find a frightening hair disturbance in my blind spot. I've heard it called a hurricane and I don't wonder for a second why. It's a giant swirly with a large eye. Who wants an extra eye in the back of her head?

The other day I found a major meteorological occurrence in the hand mirror. It started in the northernmost hair regions and moved slowly but steadily to the south, wreaking hair destruction and devastation all along the path of the storm. No doubt a category five. Would I call that a "hair-icane"? Whatever it's called, it's no small challenge to keep my head when my hair is gusting at record-breaking speeds.

Hair Peace

It happens in life too. Everything is going fine—clear with only scattered challenges. Then suddenly a storm sneaks up on you from behind. It's one of those high pressure systems that develops without much warning. Before you know it, blast the storm sirens—you're in the middle of a giant swirly.

Those kinds of disturbances happen to everyone at some time or another. Sometimes the storm hits in the form of an unkind confrontation from a friend, sometimes it's a middle-of-the-night phone call with a jolting heartache attached, or other times it's an unexpected and difficult diagnosis from the doctor or a bank statement in the mail that inspires a gasp and an extra-large swallow.

Are you feeling the full force of a vicious storm? Are your burdens weighing you down, pressure pushing you to the brink of despair?

Look to the one who is more powerful than any storm you're facing. At the moment you acknowledge your lack of power to endure, lightning-fast, his magnificent power appears to hold you up and keep you walking in the light.

Weathering the Storm

Jesus's answer to the storm is "Peace." The disciples encountered a doozy of a squall. Mark 4:37 in the Amplified called it "a furious storm of wind [of hurricane proportions]." Not a mere hairdo threat, this was a life-threatening, peace-menacing storm.

What did Jesus do? He shut it down with his "Peace, be still!"

"Then he arose and rebuked the wind, and said to the sea, 'Peace, be still!' And the wind ceased and there was a great calm" (v. 39 NKJV).

As we trust the Lord, he can speak the words "Peace, be still" into every life and into every situation. We may not necessarily evade every hair instability, but his peace can certainly help us weather out the struggle. It's all we need to make it through. Sometimes the storm still rages, but that's when his peace is all the more miraculous. We have a savior who is there when the lights go out, and who will give us peace in the midst of the storm.

Keep Your Head

So don't be surprised when a swirly struggle hits. No need to have blind spots, spiritually speaking. Look again at Isaiah 26:3: "You will keep in perfect peace him whose mind is steadfast, because he trusts in you." You can keep your head if your mind is fixed on Jesus and your heart is trusting him.

Bring your storm to Jesus, call on him, and trust him through it. He invites you every day in every situation to walk with him, to trust, to live above the circumstances—to follow him, as Paul instructed us to do—no matter what. Psalm 50:15 says, "Call to

me in times of trouble. I will save you, and you will honor me"
(NCV).

Know his "Peace, be still." Let it rule your life. In every atmospheric
condition. And while we're at it, in every shampoo and condition
too.

> And a great windstorm arose, and the waves beat into the boat, so
> that it was already filling. But He was in the stern, asleep on a pillow.
> And they awoke Him and said to Him, "Teacher, do You not care that
> we are perishing?" Then He arose and rebuked the wind, and said to
> the sea, "Peace, be still!" And the wind ceased and there was a great
> calm. But He said to them, "Why are you so fearful? How is it that you
> have no faith?" And they feared exceedingly, and said to one another,
> "Who can this be, that even the wind and the sea obey Him!"
>
> Mark 4:37–41 NKJV

USING SOUND 35
BLING JUDGMENT

Resting/Following

Well-balanced bling is a must. Heavy-duty formal necklace with light,
casual earrings? Weird. Precious stones oddly mixed with plastic
pieces? Totally off-balance. Diamonds with high-top tennies? I've
seen it done, but I'm not sure it's a good call. It's important to use
sound bling judgment.

Sound judgments are important in all areas of life. I have a good
friend whose name I've decided to herein withhold to protect the
semi-innocent. Let's call her "Rudy." Rudy is a godly, caring friend
who's always willing to go the extra mile. Her friend Lauren (not her

real name either) was upset over the fallout of an unwanted divorce and the bankruptcy proceedings that followed. To be a support, Rudy went with Lauren to her court appearance.

As you can imagine, Lauren was uncomfortable, embarrassed, and discouraged, so Rudy decided she could use some cheering up. She was determined to be Lauren's comic relief while they waited. So when the judge entered, my single friend Rudy whispered a laugh distraction to Lauren. "Mm, mm, mm—would you look at that gorgeous hunk of judge." It got a grin.

The Court Jester

"No wedding ring. That man is no doubt meant to be the father of my two cats." Another grin and a small chortle.

"Gavel-icious, judgy-wudgy." I'll see that chortle and raise you a muffled giggle.

About every minute or two, Rudy would lean over to Lauren and whisper another comment about the honored adjudicator she referred to as the "hot judge sundae."

"Raise your right hand—and I'll write my phone number on it."

"How do you feel about short engagements, Your-Honor-Hotty-Mc-Hot-Hot?"

"We'll have beautiful children—they'll have your dark curls and my good sense of judgment."

"We shall live happily ever after—whether you want to or not."

The comments kept coming. It was the most fun bankruptcy hearing Lauren had ever had. Okay, Lauren had never had a bankruptcy hearing before, but she was still having a great time. Who'd a thought?

A Motion from the Bench

As the business of the court wound down, the judge surprised everyone when he motioned to Rudy, "Could you come forward, please?" The entire courtroom probably heard her swallow.

"FOLLOW MY EXAMPLE"

"Me?"

He nodded. She sheepishly stepped up to the bench and without thinking, curtsied. "Yes sir, your honor, sir?"

"I wanted to mention that you made my day. I'm married and wasn't able to wear my ring today, but I got a kick out of your comments, and I can't wait to tell my wife."

Rudy's eyebrows were near her hairline, eyeballs bulging out of their sockets, blood pressure no doubt an impressive twenty points higher than usual. Her half-smile was frozen and a little contorted. "Beg pardon, sir?"

Hear Ye, Hear Ye . . . Um . . . I Can Hear Ye

"I'm sorry," explained the judge, "you may have noticed I mentioned that all comments between counsel and clients should be made outside the courtroom. It's because there are certain hot spots in this room that carry sound directly up here. You were in one of them, and . . . well . . . we heard everything."

Talk about "sound judgments"! His formerly ultra-dignified court officer was all but doubled over.

Rudy had a flashback of her tag "Your-Honor-Hotty-Mc-Hot-Hot" in large fluorescent letters across her brain. Mortified, she tossed the judge a mumbled, "Okay, sir. Bye, bye, sir," two more curtsies, and then grabbed Lauren and her papers and flew out of the room.

Lauren was laughing so hard she almost couldn't get herself through the courtroom door without collapsing. She landed on a bench outside, tears rolling down her face. Through all the laughter, Lauren did manage to ask, "Why did you keep curtsying? It's 'his honor,' not 'his majesty'!"

Sidebar, Your Majesty

"I *curtsied*? Tell me I didn't curtsy!" More mortification.

In the end, Rudy experienced a great deal more embarrassment than Lauren ever even thought about. And somehow, that made Lauren's day. It was actually a pretty happy ending—even if Rudy never did get to carry Judge-Cutie-Robes over any threshold.

It's a good reminder, though, that our One True Judge always hears too. He knows everything we're going through. And we can rest in his good, sound judgment. We follow in the example of Paul and ultimately the example of Jesus when we rest in him.

Peace defined is not the absence of trouble or heartache or conflict, or the absence of an unwanted divorce or an embarrassing bankruptcy. Peace is resting in God, despite it all. It's a beautiful sense of well-being through every difficulty, a knowing that you're cared for, that your eternity is settled, that God is in control and that it's okay that you're not. Sometimes it's even a chuckle in the midst of it all. Who'd a thought?

Rest Assured

You can rest, assured that the Lord has the very best in mind for you. Following the Jesus way is following the "rest" way. Jesus said in Matthew 11:29, "Take my yoke upon you and learn from me, for I am gentle and humble in heart, and you will find rest for your souls." The Amplified version describes that soul-rest as "relief and ease and refreshment and recreation and blessed quiet for your souls." I love the thought of recreation for our souls!

You don't have to carry your yoke alone. Jesus is right there beside you, offering to carry it with you. He promises you rest—and it's the sweetest, most recreational soul-rest.

In *My Utmost for His Highest*, Oswald Chambers wrote:

Are you severely troubled right now? Are you afraid and confused by the waves and the turbulence God sovereignly allows to enter your life? Have you left no stone of your faith unturned, yet still not found any well of peace, joy, or comfort? Does your life seem completely barren to you? Then look up and receive the quiet contentment of

"FOLLOW MY EXAMPLE"

the Lord Jesus. Reflecting His peace is proof that you are right with God, because you are exhibiting the freedom to turn your mind to Him. If you are not right with God, you can never turn your mind anywhere but on yourself. Allowing anything to hide the face of Jesus Christ from you either causes you to become troubled or gives you a false sense of security.[1]

Reflecting on His Peace and Rest

We're able to reflect the peace of God as we take our eyes off of ourselves and everything temporary and put them on Jesus and all things eternal. I've wondered if Paul knew his blindness was temporary when he encountered Christ on the road to Damascus. He was blind for three days. In Acts 9:12, we're told he had been given a vision that Ananias would put his hands on him and his sight would be restored. But it doesn't say when he received the vision.

Whether he knew his blindness was temporary or not, I don't think a life without sight was Paul's number one thought after his life-altering encounter. I think he was at least as busy praising God for his newfound spiritual vision, learning to trust him step by step.

We're exercising sound judgment when we focus on the spiritual and not the physical and when we rest in the God who gives peace. In his rest and peace, we can praise him, step by step, everywhere we go.

As for the Disorder in the Court . . .

In case you're wondering, Lauren is doing well and Rudy is recovering from her case of near-terminal embarrassment. We've told her to be careful where she goes, though. We're not completely convinced that *Mrs.* Judge-Cutie-Robes hasn't filed a restraining order.

> With your very own hands you formed me;
>   now breathe your wisdom over me so I can understand
>   you.

When they see me waiting, expecting your Word,
  those who fear you will take heart and be glad.
I can see now, GOD, that your decisions are right;
  your testing has taught me what's true and right.
Oh, love me—and right now!—hold me tight!
  just the way you promised.
Now comfort me so I can live, really live;
  your revelation is the tune I dance to.

Psalm 119:73–77 Message

PART 8

"AND GOD, WHO GIVES PEACE, WILL BE WITH YOU"

To Bead 36
or Not to Bead

God Is the Author of Peace

I went to a make-your-own jewelry party a few months ago. I loved it—it was a total bling-fest! Beads, beads, and more beads. There must've been an acre or two of beads. It looked like a field of jewelry seeds. I wondered if I could try planting them and shooting for my own bumper bling crop.

The gal in charge showed me how to start a necklace, and I began stringing. I strung beads until I was cross-eyed. Or maybe instead of crossed eyes they would be closer to "beady" little eyes, I'm not sure. Either way, I was totally captivated by the idea of creating my own bling. We're talking fun.

The problem was that I didn't know where to stop. I seemed to want at least one bead from each container. Big beads, little beads, shiny perfect rounds, and ruggedly interesting asymmetricals. Each little bead called to me, "Pick me!" Who was I to disappoint? When cute beads are calling, it's just too hard not to add more. I'll take one of those. And one of those. And two of those. And thirty-two of those. So much bling, so little twine!

I loaded the last bead on the necklace and got the clasp on, but when I looped it around my neck a few times, it looked like I was the victim of a multi-hive attack of angry bees. What was I, the queen bead?

And the Bead Goes On

I decided to try something smaller and started on a bracelet. But the beads still called. And I listened. "Sure, little bead—hop on!" I kept adding every manner of bead until I'm not sure it was actually a bracelet anymore. Every bead added another jingle too. I suddenly realized I could probably use the thing to call my family for dinner. And I wasn't sure how I felt about wearing a bracelet that could double as a cowbell. I got completely carried away in adding bling to more bling. Adding a little of this and a lot of that. I needed a cup of coffee. Though with or without coffee, I can still keep adding 'til the cows come home.

Believe it or not, I'm just about as bad at over-adding when it comes to accessorizing my coffee. Remember the days when you could order a cup of coffee in four syllables? A cup of coffee was a "cup-of-cof-fee." That's it. These days, coffee has been accessorized to triple its original syllabling. Or even more.

Coffee Accessorizing

Being the accessory overachiever that I am, you can imagine that I get pretty excited about coffees that can be accessorized and enhanced until they're hardly coffee anymore. I love a shot of this flavor and a dollop of that topping. Sprinkles? Sure. I just have to remember when I get up to the cash register that every syllable is about another quarter to fifty cents. A six-dollar cup of coffee? I tell you, I can do it. I can accessorize my coffee until the cows come home. And that reminds me to add cream.

Adding this, adding that—it may be overkill in a bracelet or expensive in a cup of coffee, but it can be great for life. Through our own little bling-fest in this book, we've looked at all the right things to add to our thinking—and they're all worthwhile syllables we can add to our lives. When we add godly thoughts, attitudes, mind-sets, and behaviors to our lives, then the God of peace adds the peace of God to our lives. It's a peace that adds comfort and confidence, purpose and pleasure. But the most glorious accessory to peace is the presence of its author. God is the author of peace (1 Cor. 14:33). He promises in Philippians 4:9 that he will not only add peace, but he will add his presence: "And God, who gives peace, will be with you" (CEV).

What a Designer!

I wonder if the Father ever laughs at my feeble attempts at stringing beautiful bling. My biggest hive-necklace is not even up to microscopic proportions compared to the beauty he has created. He created all beauty. What a loving thing to add! He could've created the world with no bling at all. But consider the sky alone. With a look up, we see an amazing blue with fluffy white embellishments. And he added the sun—the bling of all bling. The bright yellows, red-oranges, and even purples he dabs into a sunrise or a sunset are some of the most amazing, creative, beautiful sights in all creation.

He added beauty to beauty. In the night sky, his diamond-sparkly stars are accented all the more against the dark, velvety backdrop. The moon is like the focal piece of the night sky bling. Have you ever wondered why the Father went to so much trouble to create such beauty? If he had made the sky perpetually blah-black-and-white, we wouldn't have known the difference. But he is the maker of great beauty. I imagine love being his inspiration for every spectacular sparkle of sky-bling and every remarkable, breathtaking color he splashes throughout the earth.

All that amazing beauty is practically blah-black-and-white compared to the color he adds to our lives by his peace. The creator of everything beautiful is the creator of the peace that can fill your life with blessed color. Let his peace fill your life. Let it wash over you in the most vibrant colors of the sunset.

Add His Peace

In our flesh, we tend to add the wrong things to our lives. But every distress you carry with you, every drop of guilt and shame you've added, every worry, struggle, heartache, can be bathed in the colorful splashes of his peace. Every shameful, hurtful word you've spoken, lie you've told, person you've bruised—every time you've let yourself wake up in someone else's bed, every time you've struggled to remember the drunken revelry of the night before, every dark thought or evil action you've ever added to your life—his love and peace can wash over it all like a sunrise washing away the darkness of night.

Can you imagine looking at all the ugly things you've added to your life on your own, only to find the brilliance of the color of his love and peace? Those shames, hurts, and heartaches? You'll hardly see them. They can be completely peace-covered by the author of peace himself!

Every letter Paul wrote that is included in God's Word begins with a blessing or greeting of peace. He reminds us at every turn that Jesus is the author of peace—beginning, middle, and end of our lives—and that his peace is always available to those who love him, no matter the circumstances. We're blessed when we stay alert to what the Father has added to our lives—and alert to what we should be adding.

Hey, I think I might just stay alert with a Grande Espresso Mocha Carmel Macchiato with extra foam and chocolate sprinkles. Though the gal in charge of the make-your-own jewelry party suggested maybe I ought to try decaf.

> The Lord bless you and watch, guard, and keep you;
>   The Lord make His face to shine upon and enlighten you and be gracious (kind, merciful, and giving favor) to you;
>   The Lord lift up His [approving] countenance upon you and give you peace (tranquility of heart and life continually).
>
> Numbers 6:24–26 AMP

"AND GOD, WHO GIVES PEACE, WILL BE WITH YOU"

HIGH SOCIETY 37
ANXIETY

Worry

High society accessorizing? Who needs the pressure? I have enough trouble deciding which earrings to wear to the grocery store. Just trying to get good hair can cause enough anxiety for me.

Please excuse more hair talk, but sometimes I think of my hair as a giant accessory. Not the bows, bands, and barrettes, but the hair itself. Casual hair. Fancy hair. Do it up, do it down. And I can't deny that I change the color almost as often as I change my earrings.

Every day is a new hair day. I really never know how it's going to turn out. Some days I can strut out of the house convinced that I look very "Meg Ryan in *You've Got Mail*"—only a shade or two browner. Other days I'm just sure I'm Carrot Top—only a shade or two saner. And it's always "up in the air" whether or not all that hair gel is going to keep my hair . . . well . . . up in the air. I tend to worry I'm going to end up with some kind of pancake, horizontal force-field-looking thing happening. It's not that I don't use plenty of gel. I just never know for sure if the force is going to be with me. I call it "serendipity-do."

Worry Is a Serendipity Don't

Worry is one of those things that's about as slippery as cheap hair gel. You know, I can convince myself that worry works.

Most of the things I worry about never happen, so it must be working, right?

Not. I readily admit that I've never heard of anyone who worried successfully. As a matter of fact, here are some worry testimonials I'm quite sure you'll never, ever hear.

Worry Testimonial One: "My hair flattened out and stuck itself firmly to my head. What was I to do? But then I worried and fretted and stewed about it, and, wouldn't you know, that worry puffed my do right back into place! I didn't even need to spray!"

Worry Testimonial Two: "My son was going the wrong direction and was late coming home one evening, so I pictured him lying in countless ditches or locked up in jail and worried myself into a giant case of indigestion. Just three or four rolls of Rolaids later and, presto! That worry brought my boy right back home and put him on the straight and narrow!"

Worry Testimonial Three: "My job was iffy, my boss was out to get me, my co-workers were getting meaner by the day. But then I discovered the winning power of worry. I worried myself into a good lather, gave myself a mild cardiac episode and a couple of migraines—and it worked! Now my job is secure, my boss loves me, and we're one big happy family at work. And the insurance covers all my new medical bills!"

Worry Testimonial Four: "I was stressed about our finances. The bill collectors were making phone threats and I dreaded getting the mail. That's when I discovered worry. I lost so much sleep to extreme anxiety that I have new wrinkles that will never go away and dark circles under my eyes that no zombie could equal. In addition to the sleep problems, I even have a new ulcer. In no time, after I vexed myself into black eyes, wrinkles, and debilitating stomach pain, worry paid all my bills and gave me a handsome shopping bonus to boot! What would I have done without worry?"

Worry Is Not Your Friend

The truth is, worry does absolutely nothing good. Worry is not your friend. It's anti-peace—and it's anti-faith and anti-trust in God.

One term for "worry" comes from the Greek word that means "dividing the mind." It sounds like a wild part on a bad hair day, but it's even worse. Ever feel like worry is splitting you in two? James 1:8 says that a double-minded person is "unstable in all he does." Trying to focus on what you need to do when half of your divided mind is occupied with the object of your worry is futile. Worry leaves you with half a mind—indecisive, unfocused, unstable.

When we're worrying, we're not keeping our minds on the things Paul has instructed us to think about in our focal passage, and we're certainly missing the reality that the God "who gives peace" will be with us. We reject his presence, his peace, and his plan when we choose the worry way.

Paying for Worry in Advance

It's true that many times we worry over things that haven't even happened. Talk about a waste! Our Father divvies a large portion of grace and strength for each moment—exactly what you need. Do you realize how much of that is wasted when you worry? You're frivolously spending your grace and strength, wasting your energy, withering it all away on worry.

God's Word gives us a different choice when worry creeps in, and his is a better way. Philippians 4:6–7 says,

> Don't worry about anything; instead, pray about everything. Tell God what you need, and thank him for all he has done. Then you will experience God's peace, which exceeds anything we can understand. His peace will guard your hearts and minds as you live in Christ Jesus.

NLT[b]

Prayer instead of worry. That works. It works better than even the highest end hair gel. Exchanging worry for prayer is the way to live a life of sweet peace in Jesus. Psalm 55:22 says, "Cast your burden on the Lord [releasing the weight of it] and He will sustain you"

(AMP). Why carry around that burdensome weight of worry when we can swap it for peace?

Time to Choose

Are you feeling powerless to stop the worrying? We're instructed in the Word of God not to worry, and he will never ask us to do anything he won't empower us to do. You *can* stop living in worry. We've looked at Paul's long list of reasons to stew and fret. When he wrote the letter to the Philippians, he was in a dirty prison, facing the grim possibility of execution. His health was not great and he was constantly dealing with the immaturities of the people and churches he was called to disciple. But instead of being overcome by anxiety, Paul, inspired by the Holy Spirit of God, gives the charge for us to experience God's peace, not worry.

Don't let worry stifle what the Lord wants to do in your life. Don't let it distract you from your purpose, your calling. We're called to live the "whatsoever" life, not the "what if" life. Choose to trust the all-powerful God. Is there any situation he can't handle? No! Will anything ever happen to you that catches him by surprise? No! There's no trouble or challenge in your future that doesn't already have a huge load of his grace hanging over it, waiting for you to ask, to prayerfully trust him.

> *O Lord, teach me to choose trust over worry.*
> *Teach me to trust you with my whole heart.*

Choose Peaceful, Prayerful Trust

Don't wait for feelings. We've already seen that they can't be trusted. Start with the prayerful trust of your Father God, then watch as those feelings get on board with your choice to run to him. In Psalm 94:19, the psalmist says, "I was very worried, but you comforted me and made me happy" (NCV). Choosing the peace of God over worry is the way to find comfort and happiness.

As for my hair gel? I'm choosing not to worry about that either. I guess I'll just keep doing what I'm serendipity-doing.

> This is why I tell you: Don't worry about your life, what you will eat or what you will drink; or about your body, what you will wear. Isn't life more than food and the body more than clothing? Look at the birds of the sky: they don't sow or reap or gather into barns, yet your heavenly Father feeds them. Aren't you worth more than they? Can any of you add a single cubit to his height by worrying? And why do you worry about clothes? Learn how the wildflowers of the field grow: they don't labor or spin thread. Yet I tell you that not even Solomon in all his splendor was adorned like one of these! If that's how God clothes the grass of the field, which is here today and thrown into the furnace tomorrow, won't He do much more for you—you of little faith? So don't worry, saying, "What will we eat?" or "What will we drink?" or "What will we wear?" For the idolaters eagerly seek all these things, and your heavenly Father knows that you need them. But seek first the kingdom of God and His righteousness, and all these things will be provided for you. Therefore don't worry about tomorrow, because tomorrow will worry about itself. Each day has enough trouble of its own.
>
> Matthew 6:25–34 HCSB

Sparkle 38
and Spit-Shine

Fear

If I had a crown, I would want it to sparkle at every point and crevice, nook and cranny. Crowns are perched up there for everyone to see.

They're like reflectors for your head. Necklaces, rings, and other bling things? They're not quite the cranium spotlight a crown is.

I realize that there are reasons I'll probably never have a crown this side of glory. One is that I'm not likely destined to be queen. Not even princess. Go figure. Another is that I'm not sure I'd be willing to sacrifice my hairdo anyway. You have to have just the right do or it's crown hair for sure. Yet another reason I'll probably never have a crown? I have no idea where to buy crown polish.

I've heard all jewelry could use a cleaning now and again. How can you tell if yours needs a bit of spiffing?

Top Ten Ways You Can Tell Your Jewelry Needs Cleaning

1. Your jewelry is bigger than it used to be, but you're not sure why.
2. When you take it off the dresser to put it on, you notice it left a mark.
3. You notice it not only left a mark on your dresser, but it took the varnish off.
4. The dog tries to bury it.
5. You find a plant growing from it.
6. Flies are starting to swarm.
7. You notice a dense fog around it.
8. The EPA tries to regulate it.
9. It becomes host to several small life-forms.
10. It becomes its own life-form.

I don't want to hear my jewelry singing. That's just scary. I do try to clean mine before it starts to colonize.

I confess that I'm not as conscientious about cleaning some things as I am others. Ring cleaning always comes before necklaces, and earrings come before bracelets. I'm not sure why. I'm not as conscientious about cleaning some things around the house as I am others, either. Washing dishes comes before cleaning the floor, and cleaning the floor comes before dusting the furniture. I'm not completely sure why there either. And everything comes before windows. That I do know. It's because I don't do windows. When mine get dirty, I assume that's a sign it's time to move.

A Window of Opportunity

I have a friend who is much more window-conscious than I am. She had all new windows installed last year. She was particularly tickled about them because they tilted in for easy cleaning. She saw it as an opportunity to have perpetually clean windows. That tilt-in feature solidly sold her. Until spring cleaning time came around, that is. She got all her window-cleaning paraphernalia ready. You've never seen anyone as excited about cleaning windows as this gal. She went down her list. Bucket, sponges, squeegee—check, check, check.

The excitement dissolved, however, as soon as she tried to tilt in the first window. She clicked here and yanked there. Shoved here and twisted there. She tried no less than nine of the ten most popular wrestling moves, and that window would not budge. She couldn't get any of them to work. Before the sun went down, picture my poor friend half dangling from the roof of her two-story home washing her tilt-in windows from the outside! By the time the windows were clean, her clothes were wet and dirty, her hair was half out of her ponytail, and she was eating handfuls of chocolate chips right out of the bag.

Tilt!

Cleaning tilt-in windows from the outside hanging from a ladder. Talk about inside-out. One of the only things that could top the inconsistency would be trying to balance fear and peace at the same time. Are you yearning for peace but living all too often in fear instead? Understanding this part of Philippians 4:9 holds the answer for you: "And God, who gives peace, will be with you."

What makes the difference between living in fear and living in peace? Understanding his presence—resting in it, depending on it, trusting in his love—will dissolve fear. First John 4:18 says it plainly: "Perfect love casts out fear" (NKJV).

When you know with all your heart and soul that he is with you, fear doesn't even make sense. Hanging onto him and following him with fervor and fear won't even be an option. People who don't follow the Lord are the ones who live in fear. And why not? They're trusting in themselves. Fear actually makes sense for them. But those who follow and honor God are lionhearted—bold and courageous. Proverbs 28:1 says, "The wicked flee when no man pursues them, but the [uncompromisingly] righteous are bold as a lion" (AMP).

Step Out of Fear and Into Peace

If you've been living in fear, embrace the truth that fearful living is not God's plan for you. You can stop letting fear rule your life this very moment by grabbing on to the truth that there is nothing on this planet worthy of your fear. You can face anything, not because you have to be good enough or smart enough or cute enough, but because you follow with abandon the God of all strength. He reminds us in Genesis 28:15, "I am with you and will watch over you wherever you go." When you look at life from an eternal perspective and recognize the Lord's presence, he will fill you with his peace. Don't fear. Step into his presence and rest there until his love chases away all fear and his peace washes over you.

Remember that your future is with him. And what a future it is! Thinking about the glory to come puts fear in its place. Imagine streets of gold, gates of pearl, bling under, over, and all around—not to mention a crown that never needs cleaning. But that's not what will make heaven sweet. Our greatest joy will be living in his presence in the most tangible way and casting our crowns at the Savior's feet.

Ponder his presence and find a new birth of courage within. Take Isaiah 41:10 to heart: "So do not fear, for I am with you; do not be dismayed, for I am your God. I will strengthen you and help you; I will uphold you with my righteous right hand." The God of peace is with you—what an honor! Trust him, lean on him, love him. Wear the strength and courage he gives you like a crown of honor.

And don't fear for a second what it might do to your hair.

> I look up to the mountains—
>> does my help come from there?
> My help comes from the LORD,
>> who made heaven and earth!
> He will not let you stumble;
>> the one who watches over you will not slumber.
> Indeed, he who watches over Israel
>> never slumbers or sleeps.
>
> Psalm 121:1–4 NLT[b]

ON RING GRIPS AND 39
MIXED DIPS

Real Security

There's a fine line between a ring that flies off with every hand gesture and one that's so tight it doesn't come off even with vise grips. A loose-fitting, fly-across-the-room ring could break a lamp or put an eye out. No one wants that. I've heard a nonslip ring grip can work wonders.

Then again, blood flow to the ring finger is essential too. And when it's cut off, there is a total crisis of sizing. How many times have we had to dip a strangling ring finger in butter? And do you think that's fattening? Of course, I've also heard that—all calories aside—a butter dip here or there can be good for your skin. The finger may be a little blue, but the skin surely is soft. Hmm, if it's not too high cal, maybe I should consider a butter-dipped *face*.

Little Dippers

Even though there are a lot of dippers in my family, I am so not one of them. My family is the worst. There's not a glass of milk or cup of coffee that's completely safe from these unruly dunkers.

Personally, I think all people should eat their food and drink their drinks and never the twain should steep. I'm not sure why so many people think that their solids and liquids have to come together to make something that can no longer be classified as either.

I guess that's why I'm not a big dipper. I'm not a little dipper either. I won't dip, don't ask me. To me, dipping is pretty close to an illness. As a matter of fact, when you're soaking a cookie and mess up on the timing, you have to watch a perfectly good cookie with a composition that's reduced to mush. I call that Oreo-porosis. Vitamin-fortified milk doesn't help.

Dunk-saster

And what about when you leave your tasty little morsel even longer than too long and the entire thing caves? It's a total crisis of dunking. Do you fish for the lost cookie or donut or whatever (not exactly a high-class move), or do you have a little time of mourning and just let it go? And then when you get to the end of your drink, what do you do with the semi-solids in the last swig? Chewing your drink? That's just wrong. I think I'll always find drinking cookie pulp hard to swallow.

I don't know, maybe it's a pride thing, but I refuse to dip.

Good thing I'm not in a Naaman kind of position, huh? In 2 Kings 5, Elisha told him to dip in the river seven times to get rid of his leprosy, but Naaman wanted something fancier than your basic dunk—and because of his pride he almost missed a healing!

The world will tell you that you'll find security as you believe in yourself and trust in what you can do. That's not God's way. It's not the way to peace. Living life recognizing that the God of peace is with you brings security on a whole new level. And we can find security as we forget about depending on ourselves and become humbly obedient.

Humble Security

Pride can cause us to miss a lot of great things. Thinking we're too good to minister to this person or too important to lower ourselves to that task. Yet how often have we humbled ourselves to serve and found immense blessing in knowing that person and great reward in doing that task?

We can learn humility from the example of Jesus. There was no person too low. There was no act of service too humiliating—from washing his disciples' feet to hanging on a cruel cross.

When we line up our humility goals with the example of Christ, the humble way of life becomes something we can really sink our teeth into, so to speak.

Enough Is Enough

Do you ever feel insecurity creeping into your way of thinking? Projects that seem bigger than you are? Demands you're sure are just beyond your capabilities? Responsibilities you're sure you're underqualified for? If so, girlfriend, you're totally dipping into my side of the milk.

You want me to do what, Lord? Surely you can see that I'm too disorganized. I'm not equipped to do that. No one knows as well as you that I can be a real dingaling. I'm too undisciplined. Too easily distracted. Not fast enough. Not smart enough. Not wise enough. Not . . . well . . . not enough!

Oh my friends, Jesus has proved again and again that he is my "enough." He will be your "enough" too. I don't think there's anything that pleases him more than our coming to the end of our own "enoughs" and trusting in him to do through us what he's called us to do.

Jeremiah Was Not Enough Either

Jeremiah threw up his insecure protests in Jeremiah 1. God told Jeremiah that he had big plans for his ministry, plans the Lord had in mind for him before he knit him together in his mother's womb. But instead of saluting and diving into the job, Jeremiah's response was, "I can't speak for you! I'm too young!" (v. 6 NLT[b]). That was Jeremiah's "Lord, I'm not enough!"

God said to him, "Don't say, 'I'm too young,' for you must go wherever I send you and say whatever I tell you. And don't be afraid of the people, for I will be with you and will protect you. I, the LORD, have spoken!" (vv. 7–8 NLT[b]). And then in verse 9, God went one step further. He touched Jeremiah's mouth and said, "Look, I have put my words in your mouth!" (NLT[b]).

Where Jeremiah felt inadequate, God filled his every need. The Lord replaced his inadequacies with everything he would need to get the job done.

Do you need a security boost? Does your spirit need a lift? Get a nonslip grip on this. Strip away any pride and dip into the humility of Christ. Understand that you're not enough. Find security unsurpassed in knowing that he *is* enough. He is everything you need. His calling on your life is secure. And the peace he gives you is equally as secure. Psalm 4:8 says, "In peace I will both lie down and sleep, for You, Lord, alone make me dwell in safety and confident trust" (AMP).

So here are some ring-grip and dip tips: Skip the ego trip and get a nonslip grip. It's a sure way to secure discipleship. And that's no random quip.

> Now Naaman was commander of the army of the king of Aram. He was a great man in the sight of his master and highly regarded, because through him the LORD had given victory to Aram. He was a valiant soldier, but he had leprosy.
>
> Now bands from Aram had gone out and had taken captive a young girl from Israel, and she served Naaman's wife. She said to her mistress, "If only my master would see the prophet who is in Samaria! He would cure him of his leprosy."
>
> Naaman went to his master and told him what the girl from Israel had said. "By all means, go," the king of Aram replied. "I will send a letter to the king of Israel." So Naaman left, taking with him ten talents of silver, six thousand shekels of gold and ten sets of clothing. The letter that he took to the king of Israel read: "With this letter I am sending my servant Naaman to you so that you may cure him of his leprosy." . . .
>
> So Naaman went with his horses and chariots and stopped at the door of Elisha's house. Elisha sent a messenger to say to him, "Go, wash yourself seven times in the Jordan, and your flesh will be restored and you will be cleansed."
>
> But Naaman went away angry and said, "I thought that he would surely come out to me and stand and call on the name of the LORD his God, wave his hand over the spot and cure me of my leprosy. Are not Abana and Pharpar, the rivers of Damascus, better than any of the waters of Israel? Couldn't I wash in them and be cleansed?" So he turned and went off in a rage.
>
> Naaman's servants went to him and said, "My father, if the prophet had told you to do some great thing, would you not have done it? How much more, then, when he tells you, 'Wash and be cleansed'!" So he went down and dipped himself in the Jordan seven times, as the man of God had told him, and his flesh was restored and became clean like that of a young boy.
>
> 2 Kings 5:1–6, 9–14

40 Bling the Bells of Heaven

Knowing Jesus

I love being a woman. We normally get much better bling than the average guy—and generally more of it. And no one can argue that we get better shoes.

But I must admit that all those great accessories and cuter shoes come in a rather complicated package. They're packaged with hormones that go wacko and hair that requires a major time investment. There are those who would argue, but I'm convinced we have higher-priced clothing too. For instance, a guy can buy an entire package of underwear for what it costs for one girlie pair.

Packaged right along with unruly cellulite and higher prices on drawers are wacko hormones. I've heard some states have a waiting period on selling guns to women that corresponds to each woman's hormonal calendar. Hormones, stubborn cellulite, the agony of swimsuit shopping, and all the rest of the items on the dark side of the package came into the world when sin entered the picture. When Adam and Eve sinned, everything changed. Here's a big indicator: the pre-fall verse in Genesis 2:25 says, "They were naked and unashamed." That pretty much settles it for me. This was obviously back in the days when, if you'll forgive me, Victoria "didn't need no secret." It wasn't until after the curse of sin that Eve had to ask, "Adam, do you think this fig leaf makes me look fat?"

How do we make peace with our thighs? How can we find peace in a world of volcanic hormones and vicious spandex-laden swimsuits? Peace of every kind comes from Jesus. Adam and Eve's sin and the resulting curse on the world didn't catch God by surprise. He already had a plan in place to bring peace, to reconcile us to himself again. Ephesians 1:5 says, "His unchanging plan has always been to adopt us into his own family by bringing us to himself through Jesus Christ" (NLT[a]).

Perfectly Packaged Peace

You can experience his true and lasting peace no matter what size is written on the tag of your swimsuit. If your peace can be damaged or destroyed by any earthly challenge, then you're not getting your peace from the right source. The only source of that real and lasting peace is our heavenly Father. And we can only know the peace-giving Father through his Son, Jesus Christ.

Look again at Philippians 4:7: "And the peace of God, which transcends all understanding, will guard your hearts and your minds in Christ Jesus." Not only can we have peace with God through Christ because of the sacrificial death of Jesus on the cross, but we have available to us genuine peace for every aspect of life. It's all because of a loving Father who will guard our hearts and minds with the unexplainable peace of Jesus. Now there's a package!

The God who loves you wants to give you peace. He longs to give you the gift of his presence in your life. He wants you for his very own. What an amazing thing it is to be so very loved and wanted! He loves and wants you so much that even though you were separated from him by sin, he made a plan to grant you his peace.

We All Need Peace

There's not a one of us on earth who hasn't needed his redemptive peace. All of us have sinned. Romans 3:10 says, "There is no one righteous, not even one." But at our unloveliest, Jesus came as God's peace plan for us. "But God demonstrates his own love for us in this: While we were still sinners, Christ died for us" (Rom. 5:8).

Jesus, who had never sinned, came to earth to take the punishment for our sin so that we could have peace with a holy, sinless God. We were dressed in dirty, blingless rags of sin, yet Jesus traded places with us. And when he did, he made it possible for us to trade our rags for his own righteousness. Romans 3:23–25 says, "For all have sinned and fall short of the glory of God, and are justified freely by his grace through the redemption that came by Christ Jesus. God presented him as a sacrifice of atonement, through faith in his blood."

Three days after Jesus died, he rose from the dead. Sin has been conquered. Death is no longer something to fear. Jesus won the victory. If you will ask him to forgive your sin and come into your life, and if you will surrender control to him, he will forgive. There is no sin too big for the grace of your loving Savior to cover.

Take Hold of the Package

Give him your life. He will make you new and give you a life of mind-blowing peace. And it all comes packaged with eternal life—the promise of a future in heaven with him.

It breaks my heart when I think of the hundreds and thousands of women on a lifelong journey of desperately seeking peace—so many who never find it. Looking for peace in all the wrong places. My friend, if you have been yearning, searching, grasping, and scratching for peace, but you've not yet given your life to Christ, give up the struggle and take on the peace. There is only one way to have peace. Jesus.

Would you like to have true peace with God—peace with him that will take you into a glorious eternity? Sin annihilates the peace. Come to Jesus, let him become your peace. The very second you come to Jesus, you are at perfect peace with God the Father, and God is at peace with you. It's exactly what he desires for you, the child he adores. In addition to peace with him, as you grow in him and learn more about living his way, he gives you more and more peace for living.

The Prayer of Perfect Peace

Ready for a life of peace? Frustrated with running your life yourself and living in peaceless dissatisfaction? If you're ready to trade peacelessness for a life of eternal peace and purpose, surrender to his plan for you. Pray something like this:

> *Lord, I'm tired of the peace-struggle I just can't seem*
> *to win. I know I've sinned. I've broken your laws.*
> *Would you please forgive me? I believe you died on*
> *the cross to pay for everything wrong I've ever done.*
> *I believe you rose again, proving you have the power*
> *to save and proving you are victorious over sin and*
> *death. O Lord, I'm amazed that you love me enough*
> *to die for me. I'm humbled that you've wanted to*
> *forgive me all along. I trust you right now to forgive*
> *every sin. Thank you for your complete forgiveness*
> *and the peace I can have. I give you every part of*
> *my life, surrendering to your plan for me—whatever*
> *that may mean. Thank you for saving me.*
> *In Jesus' name, Amen.*

From the very nanosecond you ask, he forgives. And from the moment you pray that prayer and give him your life, he makes you brand, spanking new! Remember, we don't base that knowledge on feelings, so never mind what your feelings may tell you. We trust what his Word tells us—and God's Word tells us you now have the very presence of the God of peace living in you.

If you prayed that prayer for the first time, would you let someone know about it? Let a mature believer answer questions you may have, and let her help you get started in your new walk with Christ. And let me tell you, girlfriend, there is a joy-party in your honor in heaven! Luke 15:10 says, "There is joy in the presence of the angels of God over one sinner who repents" (NKJV). Share the joy-party!

A Little Note for Everyone as We Wrap Up

Never, never, never stop living in and basking in his peace. May I issue a charge to you to keep on learning to recognize those things that can destroy your peace? Lies the world tells you, neglecting God's Word, forgetting to pray, trusting emotions, ignoring sin, wallowing in guilt, having an out-of-balance self-esteem, disobedience, bitterness, hurtful words, busyness, stress, loving things instead of God, laziness, lack of purpose, complaining, focusing on difficulties, worry, fear, insecurity—so many threats to your peace. But when you recognize them, you can head them off at the peace pass! And remember at every turn that if you want to experience the peace of God, you must surrender to the God of peace. We have peace with God by faith—and it's the ultimate, overshadowing, everything-we-need peace. Romans 5:1 says, "Since we have been made right with God by our faith, we have peace with God" (NCV). *O Lord, continue to grant peace in every color, shape, and size to my sisters, as we look to you, grow closer to you, trust you more, and know you more, our most gracious God of peace!*

The secret to successfully living in peace is actually no secret at all. A deep, vital relationship with the God of peace. Pursue it. Continue to learn about him and grow in your love for him.

And let Victoria keep her secret! This is eternally better!

If you do this, you will experience God's peace, which is far more wonderful than the human mind can understand. His peace will guard your hearts and minds as you live in Christ Jesus.

> And now, dear brothers and sisters, let me say one more thing as I close this letter. Fix your thoughts on what is true and honorable and right. Think about things that are pure and lovely and admirable. Think about things that are excellent and worthy of praise. Keep putting into practice all you learned from me and heard from me and saw me doing, and the God of peace will be with you.
>
> Philippians 4:8–9 NLT[a]

"AND GOD, WHO GIVES PEACE, WILL BE WITH YOU"

NOTES

Introduction

1. Anita Renfroe, *If You Can't Lose It, Decorate It: And Other Hip Alternatives to Reality* (Colorado Springs: NavPress, 2007).

Chapter 6

1. Max Lucado, *A Love Worth Giving: Living in the Overflow of God's Love* (Nashville: Thomas Nelson, 2002), 91.

Chapter 16

1. Andrew Murray, "Consecration," *The Deeper Christian Life*, ccel.org.

Chapter 19

1. Ibid., original emphasis.

Chapter 20

1. Ibid.

Chapter 21

1. "Seeing Through Your Eyes," words and music by Andy Rhea (www.andyrhea music.com), © 2007. Used by permission.

Chapter 29

1. Oswald Chambers, *My Utmost for His Highest*, rbc.org/utmost/index.php.

Chapter 35

1. Ibid.

DISCUSSION GUIDE

Going on a Peace-Seeking Mission

Would you like to have a real and lasting peace that doesn't depend on circumstances? If you're turning to this discussion guide for your own personal study time, that's wonderful. I think you'll find it adjusts well for adding a personal application or two as you learn about his peace. Skip the "Opening It Up" opener prompts and bag a little extra food for thought by diving right into the questions for each chapter. There may be a few group-focused questions but they're easily tweakable to fit your personal reflection time.

If you're picking up this discussion guide for group discussion, well—what could be more fun and fruitful than going on a peace-seeking mission with a group of girlfriends? Enjoy the journey to peace!

Notes For the Discussion Leader

Taking a group with you as you pursue peace? Spectacular! This discussion guide should be just the ticket to give you hints and helps as you seek to help women apply some truths from God's Word about God's kind of peace, what peace is and how we can have it—and how we can hang onto it. How glorious when women can set a higher goal than merely reading a book. The higher goal? Getting personal, making it real, taking it to heart. Making his peace a reality as we live out this life in a way that pleases God the Father and adds great joy to our lives at the same time!

Whatsoever Things Are Lovely is a journey through Philippians 4:8–9. Isn't it wholly magnificent that as we look at God's Word, he can change us in such dramatic, life-altering ways? Watching women change right before your eyes, to the glory of God—could it get any sweeter? We'll be looking at the Philippians passage phrase by phrase. There are five chapters for every phrase and eight sections in all, plus an introduction.

If you would like to plan a nine-week study, you can take one section per week and add a session for the introduction. If you're able to take it a little slower, you'll find more opportunities for sharing more deeply. A chapter per week would be ideal, though you may find some are a little reluctant to make a forty-one-week commitment. Two to three chapters per week could be the perfect fit for some groups. Happily, anyone should be able to jump in at any time during the study. And also happily, there's really no wrong way to take your group through the peace study in *Whatsoever Things Are Lovely*. No doubt you can find a schedule that will perfectly fit your needs and your group's needs.

The questions in this guide are personal reflection questions designed to help us think about and fruitfully process what we've seen in God's Word. Each chapter will begin with a "Begin with a Grin" discussion starter designed to help women loosen up and laugh. Sometimes sharing on a surface level can break down barriers and free group members to later share on a deeper, more significant level. Have an answer or story ready for the opening time in case, as the leader, you might need to "open up the opener," so to speak. Several of the openers have some sort of award, trophy, or certificate. You can add one in those weeks where one is not mentioned, if you would like to. For a real hoot, put together (or ask a helper to put together) a homemade award for the best story. You'll be so surprised when you see how much the women look forward to those "Begin with a Grin" awards. If you take snapshots of the recipients and their awards each week, at your last group meeting, you can display them all in a hilarious remembrance.

As the discussion leader, you'll need to find that tricky balance of sharing enough of yourself on every level to allow your group to trust you, but not so much that you make the discussion too much "about you." If you have a close friend in the group, it's a great idea to make yourself accountable to her and ask her to honestly tell you if you're hitting that balance well.

I would encourage you to make it your goal to always be transparent. If you will be real—even if you have a struggle—your group will most often respect your genuineness and they will feel freer to share their own struggles as they come up.

What You'll Need to Do Each Week

Encourage your group to read the assigned chapter or chapters before the group meeting, but let them know that even if they get behind in reading, they still won't feel out of place coming to the discussion meetings. Reminders through phone calls or emails are great. You can divvy up those duties or ask one of your group members if they would consider being a contact person. Even with a contact person, as group leader, it's great to check in on your group whenever you can. Ask each one how you may pray for her.

As you're going through the week's assigned reading, make a few notes or observations you would like to point out or comment on during that week's discussion time. If the Lord teaches you something poignant, confronts you on an issue, or deeply moves you in some way, openly share that with your group.

May I also encourage you to make a commitment to pray for each of your group members each week? What life-changing power there is in prayer!

After you've done assigned readings and prayed for your group, look over the discussion questions. Be ready to offer some answers if the discussion needs a little charge, but again, be careful not to monopolize the chat time.

It's always fun, though certainly not mandatory, to have some snacks to offer. You can call for volunteers or put something together yourself. Doesn't chocolate almost always speak to women in a profound way? I've heard it said that good chocolates are like shoes. You can never have just one. Chocolate accessorizing!

Discussion Group Rules

You'll want to set up some ground rules for the group from the very first meeting. Here are some suggestions:

- Personal information shared within the group does not leave the group. Remind each other regularly that everyone should be able to freely share and know that no one in the group will ever betray a confidence.
- If someone shares a need or asks for prayer during a meeting, someone should volunteer right then to stop and pray for that need. Just a few sentences will be perfect.
- No cutting remarks or unkind comments to anyone in the group or about anyone outside the group. Uplifting, positive words only.
- Likewise, never correct anyone in front of the group. Belittling or embarrassing someone into changed behavior rarely works. If confrontation needs to happen it should happen in private and it should be done in love.
- If someone says something contrary to God's Word, however, let her know you respect her opinion, but also let her know in

love what the Bible does say. His truth needs to be our bottom line on every issue and every group discussion should reflect that.

Prayers for You!

Thank you again for taking on the role of discussion leader. You're making a difference in the Kingdom! Now may I pray for you?

Father, thank you for the discussion leader's availability to be used by you to touch the lives of women. I ask that you would bless her in the most marvelous way for her sacrifice of service. Lord, let her find joy in this journey that absolutely surprises her. May she come to know those in her group in a deeper way. May she see the lives of women changed by your power right before her very eyes. Would you please bring exactly the right women into her group? If there are any who don't know you in the most personal way, would you even now be drawing them to yourself? I ask that you would grant the discussion leader great wisdom from you, insight into your Word, and that you would grant her the sacrificial, Jesus-kind of love for each woman in her group. Knit hearts together as only you can do. Move and work in the lives of women in whatever way will bring you the most glory. Oh Lord, would you please take the leader, the group, all of us, into a deeper experience of your perfect peace! In Jesus' name, Amen.

DISCUSSION GUIDE

Introduction: *"Keep Your Minds,"* and All These Blings Will Be Added Unto You

Begin with a Grin: As you begin with a grin, ask your group members to guess how many pounds of jewelry she might have. Who might win the "Pound-for-Pound Blinging All Around" award?

1. According to the introduction, what are the marks of a misdirected life? As you look through the list, do you find any that you've experienced personally? Have you seen evidence of any of them in the lives of others? How do they affect the peace a person does or doesn't experience?
2. The Philippians 4 focus passage tells us to "keep our minds. . . ." What can we do to "keep" our minds instead of losing them?
3 Are you ready to reach for God's perfect peace—to experience it in a real and personal way—maybe like never before? Are you ready to seek his peace, "whatsoever" it might cost you? If you're ready, pray the prayer at the end of the introduction.

Part 1 "Keep your minds on whatever is true"

Chapter 1: Earbobs or Doorknobs?

Begin with a Grin: Ready for an earbob-to-earbob comparison? Who has the biggest earrings? Any special winners in a "Most Muscular Lobes" competition for the one with the heaviest ear-gear?

1. Read Psalm 119:165 again. What does this verse say brings great peace and keeps us from stumbling? Now read Deuteronomy 32:1–2 as a personal message from your heavenly Father right to you.

2. Are you ready to accept the challenge to put away a casual reading style and dig in to God's Word if you haven't before? If you've already been committed to reading the Bible and applying it to your life, are you ready to ask him to take you even deeper? As you commit to studying his Word, get ready for a changed life and new peace!

3. If you haven't yet done it, would you ask him right now to give you the discipline to grow closer to him through his Word? He'll even give you the want-to. Those are prayers he longs to answer. Ask.

Chapter 2: Ruby-rooter

Begin with a Grin: What's the funniest thing your kids or someone you've known has ever swallowed? Three cheers for the winner of the "I Find That Hard to Swallow" award!

1. Have you or has someone you've known ever swallowed the lie that to be happy you have to be gorgeous? What affect does that belief have on a person's peace level? On her self-value? On her happiness in general? On her fruitfulness for Christ? Read Psalm 139, as the chapter suggests, and spend time thinking about what God thinks of us—and of you, personally.

2. What is your take on how to find fulfillment in life? What common misconceptions about finding fulfillment and hap-

piness do you commonly see in others? How does it affect their lives?

3. According to this chapter, what should we consume instead of swallowing lies? What difference does that make in how we see others and in how we see our mission in life? What do we need to know about who we are—and whose we are—and what happens when we understand those truths?

Chapter 3: Cha-Ching Bling

Begin with a Grin: Brag on your bargains! Whether accessories or some other treasure, who gets to be labeled this meeting's smartest shopper?

1. According to this chapter, reading God's Word is not only about the memorization of facts, but what else happens when we make reading the Bible a habit? Are there places of growth you can point to in your spiritual life that are a direct result from staying consistent in reading the Word? What are some of them?

2. As you analyze your schedule, do you see something that needs to go so that you can give your quiet time with the Lord a greater place of prominence?

3. What do you think are the biggest hindrances to keeping your time with the Lord every day? Think of some practical, concrete ways you can creatively get past those hindrances and carve out that special time. Ask the advice of others if you need a little extra help.

Chapter 4: Magnum Opal

Begin with a Grin: "The Most Musical Accessory" award goes to the one who can produce the loudest or most interesting jewelry sounds.

1. Is embracing the "quiet" of a quiet time a challenge for you? Try a little Psalm 46:10 "be still and know that I am God"

time this week. Invite his presence into your day. What do you think you can hear/learn/experience in the quiet of the quiet time?

2. Try going through the "Rev Up" outline on your own. Which section is the most challenging? Which is the most rewarding?

3. What do you think "Use it UP" means? How can the "up" direction revolutionize a person's life?

Chapter 5: Supplementation of Ornamentation

Begin with a Grin: Who has the funniest story about a good outfit gone bad? Leaving sparkling trails? Molting?

1. What does it mean to "pray without ceasing" in 1 Thessalonians 5:17? How does that translate into everyday life?

2. Are there some changes you need to make in your prayer life? Do you need to "begin"—or maybe "begin" again? If you don't already have an effective prayer routine, go through each letter of the "BEGIN" outline, making each a part of your prayer time. Will you make a commitment to "begin again" each morning for two weeks?

3. How does a consistent, meaningful, intimate prayer life affect our peace?

Part 2 "Keep your minds on whatever is . . . pure"

Chapter 6: As the Ring Turns

Begin with a Grin: If your life were a soap opera, what would the title be? Who gets the "Drama Queen" award for the cleverest title?

1. What does a life look like when emotions are ruling? Can you think of a time when your life looked like that? How much peace were you experiencing?

2. How does our thought-life impact what happens in our emotions? In our actions and reactions? In our walk with Christ? In the peace we experience or don't experience?

3. Do you ever fall into the habit of thinking that you're a victim of your thoughts and that you have no control? What can you do to rein in any of those stray thoughts?

Chapter 7: Bling Radar

Begin with a Grin: What is the funniest, weirdest or most "intense" thing you've ever lost? Who wins "The Biggest Loser" award?

1. When someone experiences spiritual misdirection, in addition to thinking about it, what does that person need to do? Have you experienced that?

2. Have you ever had to come face-to-face with your sin, feeling like a real loser? How many steps does it take to go from Loser-ville to a renewed fellowship with the heavenly Father? What does that require? Where does it lead?

3. Read the Romans passage at the end of the chapter again. List a handful of life-changing results that happen as you take this passage to heart.

Chapter 8: When You've Seen One Enclosed Shopping Center, You've Seen a Mall

Begin with a Grin: What's the weirdest thing you've ever tried on in a store outside the dressing room? What's the weirdest thing you've seen someone else try on? What about inside the dressing room? Have you ever laughed out loud?

1. Has there ever been a time in your life when you didn't have many friends? Were you lonely?

2. Has there been a time that you experienced a loneliness that you knew was the result of your own disobedience to God? How do the two types of loneliness contrast and compare?

3. When our sin results in a feeling of soul-loneliness, what is the fix? How often do we need that fix? Is there anything you need to deal with right now?

Chapter 9: Bling, Bling—Hello?

Begin with a Grin: Have you seen any outrageous cell phone decorations? Who might win the "No Need to be a Phone-y" award for the most bizarre cell phone accessory?

1. When we leave guilt to fester, what are the results in our lives? How fruitful is a life consumed with guilt?
2. Read the passage at the end of the chapter (Hebrews 10:19–23). What are the key points of this passage? What are its heart messages?
3. Is there guilt hindering you that you need to get rid of? Are you ready to trade guilt for peace? According to the passage in Hebrews 10 what makes us clean? How reliable is that cleansing and how does that affect your guilt?

Chapter 10: Buttons and Boas

Begin with a Grin: Is there someone who has a scarf trick up her sleeve? Who wins the most creative "Scarf-i-gami" award for the best or most original scarf tip?

1. According to this chapter, what is it that makes us special? What impact does this thought have on our thinking when we're too full of pride? What impact does it have when we're struggling with feelings of worthlessness?
2. Where does "other-esteem" fit into our thinking? If you had to try to sort out the percentage of your thoughts that were others-directed, how would it measure up to the percentage of thoughts that are self-directed? Where do we find balance?
3. Have you prayed the prayer toward the end of this chapter? What difference do you think this kind of prayer can make?

Part 3 "Keep your minds on whatever is . . . right"

Chapter 11: Is That a Necklace or a Disco Ball?

Begin with a Grin: "The Disco Medallion" award goes to the one who brings the most out-of-the-box necklaces.

1. According to Colossians 3, how do we get to that place of right living? How does this affect our peace?
2. Under "Peace-wear," we're told we have a part to play in how much peace we do or don't experience. What is our part?
3. If you had to give yourself a grade on how well you're letting his peace rule, what would your grade be? What do you think an "A" requires?

Chapter 12: All That Glitters Is Not Bullion

Begin with a Grin: What are some of your most challenging complex tasks? Which ones seem aggravatingly over your head? Any award-winners for the "Can Hardly Set My Own Oven-timer" prize?

1. Is there a difference between thinking right, doing right, and becoming a *slave* to right? If so, what is the difference?
2. According to this chapter, how do we corner the market on the peaceful, good life? Have you made the concept of "freedom through slavery" part of your thinking?
3. What/who are you a slave to—sin or Christ? What would your life be like if you chose the other?

Chapter 13: A Little Jaded

Begin with a Grin: What's the worst thing you've ever smelled? Who wins the "Stench-a-Rama Mama" award for the best stink-story?

1. How does doing right proclaim the mighty acts of the Lord and declare his praise?

2. Have you ever encountered a person who tried to instruct you in right living but wasn't living it themselves? What kinds of feelings did that stir up? How does it affect your own desire to live what you believe?

3. If you have children, how do you think you're doing in offering them an example of thinking right and living right? Is your relationship with your heavenly Father one that is so real, exciting, and vital that it makes others want what you have?

Chapter 14: Taking Our Accessories at Face Value

Begin with a Grin: What's the most riotously extreme cosmetic procedure you've ever heard of? Can you think of one that would be even funnier?

1. According to the Word of God, when your heavenly Father looks at you, what does he see? How does that affect what you see? Does what you see in yourself line up with what the Father sees in you? How does it compare with what society tells us is beautiful?

2. When you look at your life and examine how you see and treat others, do you see a demonstration of the grace of the Father? Do you notice areas where you could/should exercise more grace? Where could you find the ability to do that?

3. How could the information in this chapter affect the sense of peace you experience? How could it affect the peace you experience with others?

Chapter 15: Shining Time

Begin with a Grin: Have you ever had an outfit that seemed so right go oh so wrong? Who might win the "Outfit from the Wrong Galaxy" award?

1. Why do you think it can be so easy to let negative lines of thinking sneak into our regular thought patterns? Do you think it's easier to think negatively than it is to dwell on the positive?
2. Read through the things we're instructed to think about in the focus passage of the book, item by item. Do you see each one represented in your thoughts? Would you be willing to read the passage every day for two weeks and purposefully come up with thoughts that represent each item in Paul's list?
3. How might dwelling on this passage every day for two weeks affect your thought patterns in a permanent way? How might it affect how you think about and respond to others?

Part 4 "Keep your minds on whatever is . . . holy"

Chapter 16: Ink-bling

Begin with a Grin: Who can bring the most unusual pen? "The Write Stuff" award goes to the wildest writing utensil.

1. What are some specific ways steering our lives away from impurity results in a life with fewer messes?
2. According to 2 Timothy 3:16–17, how can we know how to live in holiness, think in holiness, and stay away from sin?
3. What do we learn from Jonah? Have you ever found yourself in a Jonah-type "whale" of a mess? What does it take to get from disobedience and the peace-less life to a life full of the contentment-producing presence of the Lord?

Chapter 17: Turn On the Bling

Begin with a Grin: Have you ever dressed in the dark and come into the light surprised by what you were wearing? The "Most Enlightened" award goes to the one with the best story.

1. How can we keep our lives "well-lit"? Where do we find perfect light?
2. What is our calling from Philippians 2:15? What is it that makes us shine? What are some ways we see the Enemy counterfeiting the real light? How can the counterfeit be exposed?
3. What are some specific things you can do to light up your life? What kinds of choices will those things require from you?

Chapter 18: Looking at Life through Peace-Colored Glasses

Begin with a Grin: Who wins the "I Can Hardly Believe My Eyes" award for the wildest, cutest or funniest pair of glasses? Any good stories about the strangest place you've left your glasses?

1. What are some sad or strange ways we see people searching for peace? How many people have you seen giving all their energies to the search but never finding it?
2. What is the difference between seeking peace and seeking happiness?
3. What is our charge in 1 Peter 1:13–16? What is your response to the call?

Chapter 19: The Accessory Pool

Begin with a Grin: What is your funniest outdoor experience? Who might be your group's designated "Survivor Woman"?

1. What are some specific examples of pursuing peace by fleeing sin?
2. How does trusting in yourself to "get good" compare with capturing every thought and giving it to Christ (2 Corinthians 10:5)?
3. How do we know when to flee sin and when to stand and fight? Does your answer to this question call you to any particular action?

Chapter 20: The Long and Short of a Good Necklace

Begin with a Grin: Time to get out the yardstick and see who wins the "Mile-long Necklace" award. Think your accessories will measure up?

1. As you read Andrew Murray's quote under the "God's Longing" subhead, what do you think "the call of a loving Father" is all about?
2. Have you ever spent time dwelling on the sweet fact that your holy God desires to dwell in you? How does thinking on these things affect keeping our minds set on holy thinking?
3. Read the passage at the end of the chapter again. According to this passage, who changes your way of thinking? How does that happen? Has it happened to you?

Part 5 "Keep your minds on whatever is . . . friendly and proper"

Chapter 21: Accessory to the Crime

Begin with a Grin: The "Fine Taste in Jewelry" award goes to the one who brings the funniest edible accessory. Skittles for everyone—in every color!

1. What does a "1 Peter 3:8–9" kind of love look like? What are some practical ways living out this passage shows up in a person's life?
2. Are there people in our society who are difficult to "see," as this chapter defines seeing? Who are they? Are there people in your life who are difficult to see?
3. Are there changes you may need to make in the way you respond to these people? If so, what are the changes? What are some specific ways you can love those you already see and ways you can notice more those you haven't?

Chapter 22: Bling It On

Begin with a Grin: Who can come up with the funniest, most creative idea for thigh camouflage?

1. Have you ever witnessed someone giving or serving in a "radical surrender" kind of way? Have you ever given with that kind of surrender?
2. Have you ever witnessed someone giving or serving in the midst of their own crisis, pain, or struggle? What effect did the person's sacrifice have on you and others who saw it?
3. Re-read James 3:17–18 in *The Message*. Which item in the list of instructions comes most naturally? Which is most difficult for you? Can you think of ways you can take advantage of your strengths and strengthen weak areas?

Chapter 23: On Pearls and Swine

Begin with a Grin: Who wins the "Name Game" prize for naming names? What's the funniest, strangest name you've ever heard?

1. Have you ever experienced a time when you didn't have a lot of friends? What did you miss most?
2. Have there been times you've had to actively reach out, offer friendship to another, and take some risks? If so, what were the results?
3. Why is forgiveness so important in our relationships? How does whether or not a person forgives affect the level of peace that person experiences? Is there anyone you need to forgive?

Chapter 24: Silver Lining

Begin with a Grin: How about a "Not-So-Silver Lining" award for the one who has the most bizarre makeup or accessory surprise story?

1. What's the difference between being "friendly and proper" to everyone and to truly investing yourself in a friendship? What are the risks in each? What are their unique rewards? How does God's instruction apply to each?
2. What are some instances that might pop in a relationship that would encourage you to set boundaries? What kind of boundaries are appropriate for which kinds of situations?
3. Describe the differences in friendships/relationships with believers and those with unbelievers. What is our calling in each kind of relationship?

Chapter 25: Do Your Ears Hang Low?

Begin with a Grin: What's the wildest, weirdest, wackiest chewing gum situation you've seen or heard? The "Stick with It" prize goes to the one with the best story.

1. Ask the listed questions under "Word Qs" again. How different would our world be if all of us filtered our speech through those questions? Would our friendships be different? Would our homes? How?
2. Do you ever allow sneaky negative or gossip-filled words to steal your peace? Where do those negative, gossipy words come from? Where do loving words of peace come from?
3. Are you ready to ask the Lord to guard your every word, and to fill each word with truth, love, wisdom, encouragement, joy, and blessing?

Part 6 "Don't ever stop thinking about what is truly worthwhile and worthy of praise"

Chapter 26: Bling-less in St. Louie

Begin with a Grin: Have you ever forgotten an important part of your getting-ready process? Confess and chuckle. Have you seen others who obviously forgot something important as they were readying?

1. Hustling and bustling? How do we know for sure we're too busy?
2. Is there any busyness you think might be pushing your heavenly Father out of your day? If so, what needs to go? Are you ready to put your schedule on the altar and make sure your agenda lines up with his?
3. Have you prayed through your schedule? Are you ready to? Read Psalm 90:12 again and ask him to help you grow in wisdom.

Chapter 27: Keeps Me Blinging as I Go

Begin with a Grin: Who wins the "Brown Thumb" award for the worst-looking plant? Does anyone have a story about a good plant gone bad?

1. What are the two different kinds of stresses? Have you experienced or are you experiencing one or both? If so, which one?
2. In the "How Should We Respond to Stress?" section, we're given some suggestions for practical steps toward de-stressing. What are those suggestions? Are there other stress-relievers that work for you? What is your favorite way to unwind? When was the last time you did that?
3. How does Isaiah 26:3–4 affect our de-stressing techniques? Can you tell about a time God was your rock and lavished peace on you during a stressful time?

Chapter 28: Virtual Gems

Begin with a Grin: What is the weirdest or funniest thing you've received via email? Is there anything in your box that might win the "Now That's Worth Printing Out" prize?

1. Read the passage from Psalm 105 at the end of the chapter. Underline all the verbs. What do these words call us to do?
2. When was the first time you heard the gospel? When did you respond? Remember and rejoice. Who shared with you?
3. You can share the good news of salvation through Christ using verses from Romans. If you've never mapped out the Roman Road, would you consider marking these verses in your Bible so you can share them with someone? Even if you've read and memorized them, read them again right now. What a blessing! Romans 3:23; Romans 3:10–18; Romans 6:23; Romans 5:8; Romans 10:9; Romans 10:13; Romans 5:1; Romans 8:1; Romans 8:38–39

Chapter 29: Bling 911

Begin with a Grin: The "Bring It On Home" award goes to the one with the best, craziest, or funniest vacation story.

1. What happens when a person's peace is wrapped up in what she has or doesn't have? How does Ecclesiastes 5:10 fit in?
2. Describe your worth as a believer in Christ using only scripture.
3. Have you ever met a person whose self-worth was completely wrapped up in things? How much peace did that person experience? If that person asked for your input, after studying God's Word and looking at this chapter, what would you say?

Chapter 30: Engineering the Earrings

Begin with a Grin: The "La-Z-Gal" award goes to the one who comes up with the best invention idea for lazy people.

1. Tell how kicking back for some extended laziness sounds peaceful, but actually can bring about the exact opposite.

2. Where should our real rest come from? Have there been times in your life when your rest came from some other source? How much peace did you experience?

3. What do you think is the key to resting when we need to rest and working when we need to work?

Part 7 "You know the teachings I gave you, and you know what you heard me say and saw me do. So follow my example."

Chapter 31: Friend or Faux?

Begin with a Grin: Have you ever made your own brooch? Would you like to give it a try for a giggle? A "Who Can We Pin This On?" prize for the most imaginative homemade pin.

1. What would happen if we decided to follow someone who wasn't closely and obediently following Christ?

2. Have you ever met a Christian so genuine you desired to imitate her? Describe those things you most admire about her. Have any of those qualities become more evident in your own life? As you have imitated her example, have you noticed becoming an example to others?

3. Do you think there may be those who are following you? How can you ensure that you're leading in the right direction?

Chapter 32: Improper Gem Shopper

Begin with a Grin: What bizarre occurrences have you seen while shopping? Have you encountered unusual people doing unusual things? Have you ever *been* one of the unusual people doing unusual things?

1. What does it look like when someone lets negative emotions take over? How can we make sure we're not ruled by our emotions?

2. What does Paul mean when he says in 2 Corinthians 12:10, "For when I am weak, then I am strong"?

3. How difficult is it to praise the Lord when you're hurting, persecuted, overwhelmed, frustrated? What does it say about us when we can praise the Lord through it all?

Chapter 33: Accessing the Accessories

Begin with a Grin: Who might win the "That Just Doesn't Compute" award for the funniest computer mistake? A computer boo-boo someone else had made? Other computer catastrophes?

1. What happens when a new Christian never "forgets" the old way—never gets rid of old habits and old ways of thinking?

2. With what are we supposed to replace those old ways?

3. How much peace will a person experience if they keep on following that old path? How much satisfaction? Is there anything you still need to reprogram?

Chapter 34: Apparel Peril

Begin with a Grin: Who wins a "Hair-raising Peril" recognition for the wildest hair story? Got pictures?

1. What did Jesus say to calm the storm in Mark 4:39? How can those words affect a person's life?

2. Can you think of a time in your life when Jesus calmed your storm? Can you think of a time when he gave you peace in the midst of the storm, but the storm raged on? What was special about each?

3. When you're weighted down with pressures and burdens and at the brink of despair, what can you do?

Chapter 35: Using Sound Bling Judgment

Begin with a Grin: What's the most hilarious miscommunication you can remember? Are there any great stories you've "overheard" about "overhearing"?

1. How can we focus on the spiritual instead of the physical when there are difficulties in our lives?
2. How does Jesus carry your yoke? Is there a burden you're carrying now? Are you ready to ask Jesus to carry it?
3. Is there a friend you can come alongside as she carries her burden? Will you encourage her to let Jesus carry it?

Part 8 "And God, who gives peace, will be with you"

Chapter 36: To Bead or Not to Bead

Begin with a Grin: Who has a favorite coffee the whole group would love? The "Love It a Latte" award goes to the most creative coffee combo.

1. Which of the beautiful aspects of God's creation most inspires you? Think about the breathtaking beauty of his design—his gift to you—and let it lead you to praise him.
2. As you praise him, praise him as well for the peace he offers. Peace is his amazing gift, too. Read Numbers 6:24–26 at the end of the chapter.
3. Is there any worry, guilt or heartache you've been holding on to? Are you ready to let his peace wash over it all? What happens when his peace washes over our sorrow?

Chapter 37: High Society Anxiety

Begin with a Grin: What's the worst hair product you've ever tried? Who might win the "Dippety-Don't" award for the wildest hair or products story?

1. How do we pay for our worry in advance?
2. Do you know anyone who is living the "what if" life instead of the "whatsoever" life? Or are you the one living a life of worry? What might a person miss who spends much of her time worrying and fretting?
3. Pray through Philippians 4:6–7, asking the Lord to help you pray instead of worry and asking him to move you toward a worry-free existence where his peace guards your heart and mind.

Chapter 38: Sparkle and Spit-Shine

Begin with a Grin: The "Sparkle-mania" award goes to the person who has the most interesting housecleaning story. Come on. Share your dirt.

1. According to this chapter, what makes the difference between living in fear and living in peace? Describe the life lived in fear and compare and contrast it with the peace-filled life.
2. Why is it that thinking about our eternal future with Christ chases away fear?
3. Are there fears that have crept into your life? Are you ready to deal with them the Proverbs 28:1 way?

Chapter 39: On Ring Grips and Mixed Dips

Begin with a Grin: Who might take the "I'm Just Trying Not to Be a Crumb" prize for the most riotous cookie-dunking story? Other noteworthy food disasters?

1. How can pride cause us to miss opportunities, blessings, and fruit? What other things can pride cause us to miss?
2. What are some specific moments of humility Christ demonstrated as he gave us the example of his perfect humility? What are ways that we can show that same kind of humility?
3. How can humility bring security, even though they seem so opposite?

Chapter 40: Bling the Bells of Heaven

Begin with a Grin: The "Package It Up" award goes to the one who won the most awards through the *Whatsoever Things Are Lovely* study! Which one was your fave?

1. What is the one and only way to have peace?
2. Have you ever prayed a prayer like the one under the section titled, "The Prayer of Perfect Peace"? Do you remember a time when the God of peace specifically gave you the gift his peace and his presence in your life through his son, Jesus Christ? If not, are you ready to pray that prayer? If you've already given the Lord your heart, celebrate the sweet salvation you have and the peace you now experience with God through Christ.
3. Did you accept the challenge at the end of the chapter? The charge is to never top living in and basking in his peace and to keep on learning to recognize those things that can destroy your peace. Wrap up by reading Philippians 4:8–9 from the *New Living Translation.*

And may the God of peace be with you all!

Rhonda Rhea is a humor columnist and has written hundreds of articles for *HomeLife, Today's Christian Woman, Marriage Partnership, ParentLife,* and dozens more publications. Also a radio personality, she is a frequent guest of Focus on the Family's *Weekend Magazine* and *Audio Journal.* The author of several books, including *I'm Dreaming of Some White Chocolate, High Heels in High Places, and The Purse-uit of Holiness,* Rhonda and her husband, Richie, live in Troy, Missouri, with their five children. She invites you to visit her website at www.rhondarhea.org.

Laughter and Spiritual Substance for Wome

high heels **in** high places

walking worthy in way cute shoes

rhonda rhea

"Reading this book was like taking a walk with a very good friend who helped me enjoy the journey while leading me into a deeper relationship with God."

—**Carol Kent**, speaker; author, *A New Kind of Normal*

Ɽ **Revell**
a division of Baker Publishing Group
www.RevellBooks.com

in Hot Pursuit of Shoes, Handbags, and Holiness

Rhonda Rhea

the Purse-uit of Holiness

Learning to Imitate the Master Designer

discussion guide included

With sharp wit and keen insight, Rhea takes women who are on the lookout for the perfect spiritual life into an in-depth but always entertaining study of 1 Peter 1:15–16.